Also by Bruce Larson

Luke, Communicator's Commentary, vol. 3
There's a Lot More to Health Than Not Being Sick
Risky Christianity
The Whole Christian
The One and Only You
Ask Me to Dance
No Longer Strangers
The Emerging Church
Dare to Live Now
Thirty Days to a New You
Setting Men Free
Living on the Growing Edge
Believe and Belong

With Keith Miller:

The Edge of Adventure
Living the Adventure
The Passionate People: Carriers of the Spirit

Bruce Larson

Wind & Fire

Living Out the Book of Acts

WORD BOOKS
PUBLISHER
WACO, TEXAS

A DIVISION OF
WORD, INCORPORATED

Unless otherwise marked, all Scripture quotations are from The Revised
Standard Version of the Bible, copyrighted 1946, 1952, © 1971, 1973 by the
Division of Christian Education of the National Council of the Churches of
Christ in the U.S.A., and used by permission.

Library of Congress Cataloging in Publication Data

Larson, Bruce.
  Wind and fire.

  1. Bible. N.T. Acts—Sermons. 2. Presbyterian
Church—Sermons. 3. Sermons, American. I. Title.
BS2625.4.L29 1984   226'.606   84–5119
ISBN 0–8499–0364–5

Printed in the United States of America

CONTENTS

A Preliminary Word

I am always embarrassed on the occasions when I am asked for advice on writing a book. I don't actually consider myself a writer, even though this is my seventeenth published book. I know what "writers" are like. One of my children is a professional writer, as is one of my closest friends. Writers love to write and live to write. Writing absorbs them totally. They would write whether or not their writings are ever published. As for me, I would never write another word if it were not going to be published.

All this is by way of background for how this book came into being. I have two qualities that motivated me to write this book, and indeed all the others as well. I am someone with a consuming curiosity about life and faith, and I love communicating any helpful insights I learn that might benefit someone else. Perhaps that is the purpose of most nonfiction books. The writer is attempting to transmit something of value to the reader.

At any rate, when I am pressed to give advice to aspiring authors, I tell them that, ideally, a book should be a dialogue between the writer and the reader. I suggest that he or she picture one particular person that he/she knows and write the book to that person, to imagine that person sitting across the desk and to aim every sentence at that audience of one.

This book was born out of my desire to rediscover the origins of the church and the Spirit's strategy as it is revealed in the Book of Acts. I am convinced that the church the Holy Spirit is creating could be the most relevant and the most powerful institution in our society. The Book of Acts provides mind-exploding, life-changing new ways of appropriating that power to be the church to one another and to be the church in the world. I do not believe in a capricious God, yet I am aware that, at the grass roots level, churches vary greatly in terms of their ministry and mission and their impact on society. What makes the difference? I believe the Book of Acts gives us some guidelines for the kind of effectiveness we want to achieve as God's people working through the vehicle of the local church.

That will be the overall message of this book, but beyond the message, God has provided me with an ideal partner for the dialogue. My church family in Seattle, the members of the University Presbyterian Church, are often way ahead of me in living out some of the fresh, new insights in Acts, and they are always eager to experiment with anything that may have been overlooked. They have been ideal partners in dialogue for the twenty-one sermons that are the basis for this book. What we have discovered together, we are now trying to appropriate and apply.

However, a series of sermons does not make a book. My wife and best friend, Hazel, is also my editor. There would be no book without her. Her efforts are obvious on every page and every line.

Assisting Hazel has been my administrative assistant at University Presbyterian Church, Gretha Osterberg. On weekends and in the wee hours she has typed, corrected, researched and encouraged—a teammate without price.

Another colleague and friend, Hal Jaenson, had the job of

transcribing the original sermons from tapes. His help was invaluable and his friendship a gift.

Finally, my old friend, Ernie Owen, vice president and editorial director at Word, believed in this book before it was a book and encouraged me to produce it. I am grateful for his help and support.

As you read this book, I pray that the Spirit Himself will give you His wind and fire. Expect new insights, new strategies, new power and new courage to follow where He leads. Know that you are a part of God's underground revolutionary army, those who are redefining the church in our time all across the world.

INTRODUCTION

Redefining the Church

ACTS 1:1–5; 2:1–4

One day as I was looking for a football game on the car radio, I tuned in by chance on one of those marvelous art forms that I hope will never disappear—a sermon by an old-fashioned southern revival preacher. He was really giving it to us. If you've never lived in the South and attended a revival meeting full of enthusiasm and noise and all kinds of unexpected happenings, you have missed a great experience.

I had an old friend who was that kind of a preacher. He loved to expound on esoteric and obscure texts. One Sunday evening he said, "Tonight I'm going to explain to you the unexplainable. I am going to define the undefinable. I'm going to ponder the imponderable. I'm going to unscrew the inscrutable." And he proceeded to do just that. I'm especially reminded of that as we focus on wind and fire, the Holy Spirit and His Church, and the exciting account of that which we find in the Book of Acts. Perhaps in these coming chapters we can unscrew the inscrutable.

I think one of the pivotal theologians of the twentieth century, liberal or conservative, Protestant or Catholic, was Emil Brunner. He had a brilliant mind and a great love for the Master, and years ago he wrote a little book called *The Misunderstanding of the Church*. It didn't sell too well, but it's one of my favorites. He was asking, "What is the church? That is the great unsolved question of Protestantism." As we study the beginnings of the church from the Book of Acts, I hope we can find the power and the wisdom of the Spirit to redefine this marvelous and mysterious organism which in our time seems to be a proverbial sleeping giant. The church needs to be redefined in every age lest it be lost in the wrappings of contemporary culture.

One September my wife and I were on study leave in Greece and thought it especially appropriate to have our daily devotions from 1 and 2 Thessalonians, letters Paul wrote to the church in Thessalonika, to help them understand who they were as members of Christ's Body and what their mission was. By contrast to that early church, the church in Greece today seems to be a collection of buildings that serve almost as museums full of gorgeous icons and art work, incense, lights and candles. Invariably, some very ancient ladies seem to serve as caretakers. But almost no one comes. The average Greek is content to observe religious holidays and fast days. Seemingly, the traditions of the faith are all that remain in this land in which the church took root some two thousand years ago with such vitality and power. Coming from another culture, we immediately perceived the enormous gulf between the first century church that we read about in Thessalonians and today's churches, and we were shocked. But according to Brunner, the church all around the world is suffering from the same misunderstanding of its identity, purpose and mission.

Any number of our country's structures and institutions are suffering from a similar misunderstanding of their identity and purpose. For example, the judicial system, which exists to insure justice and equality to all people, has become corrupted and needs to be redefined. No less a figure than Warren Burger, our Supreme Court's Chief Justice, is saying that we need to reevaluate and reform the whole process of litigation so that it may better serve our citizens. In terms of our government, each new administration is faced with the question of what government should do and be.

An August 1982 publication carried an excerpt of a talk by Jerrold Michael, Dean of Public Health at the University of Hawaii, urging us to back off and redefine what medicine might be in the decades to come. He reports that since 1950 the amount of money spent per person on health care has risen 1,100 percent. It is presently elevenfold more costly than it was in 1950 to obtain health services. However, the incidence of mortality and disability has not decreased one bit since 1955. We are spending ever-increasing amounts of money with no better results. This medical man, speaking to his colleagues, explained that 50 percent of all illnesses are caused by chosen life style, 20 percent are caused by environmental factors, 20 percent are biophysical, and only 10 percent can be attributed to the quality of health care. Nevertheless, we spend 1,100 percent more money on this 10 percent of the problem with no better results.

Columnist Sidney Harris wrote recently about the corruption of great ideas. He said we have perverted Darwin's theory of the survival of the fittest to mean that the strong and aggressive will come out on top. Actually, Harris reminds us, survival of the fittest means that those who can adapt to change will survive. Similarly, we have perverted Freud's theories on the problem of repression to mean "Do whatever feels good." Freud never advocated that, but we have somehow made him the high priest of license in the area of our appetites. Harris also mentioned Einstein, the physicist who advanced the theory of relativity, pointing out that we have interpreted this theory to mean that there is no truth and everything is relative. Einstein, of all people, believed in scientific certainties and absolute natural laws.

In 1976 one of my favorite authors, Saul Bellow, received the Nobel Prize for Literature. He took that opportunity to make these remarks about current books, "How weary we are of them. How poorly modern writers represent us people. The picture they offer no more resembles us than we resemble the restructured reptiles and other monsters in a museum of paleontology. We are much more limber, versatile, better articulated, there is much more to us, we all feel it. The struggle that convulses us makes us want to simplify, to reconsider, to eliminate the tragic weakness which prevents writers—and readers—from being at once simple and true. . . . A heap of mummies, the most respectable leaders of the intellectual community, have laid down the law. We must not make bosses of our intellectuals."

Bellow, one of our leading intellectuals, is urging us to do our own thinking and press for simple truths. And I would add to his warning by saying, "Let's not make bosses of our theologians." The definition of the church is too important to be left to theologians. We who are believers *are* the church, and we need to apply our minds and hearts to understand who and what God is calling us to be. To do so we have no more reliable source than the Book of Acts.

William Barclay, well-known scholar and author of many commentaries, calls the Book of Acts the most important single book in the New Testament. And for Christians, I imagine that would make it the most important book in the whole Bible. Its author, Luke, is also the author of one of the four Gospels, and I believe it is significant that these are the only New Testament books written by a Gentile. Luke is also a physician and his language reflects that. For example, when Jesus is quoted as saying, "It's more difficult for a rich man to enter the kingdom of God than for a camel to move through the eye of a needle," the other Gospel writers use a word denoting a sewing needle. Luke uses the word for a suture needle, the type used in surgery. How amazing that a Gentile physician should have written what Barclay calls the most important book in the New Testament.

The English translation for the title of this book is "The Acts of the Apostles," in my opinion an erroneous title, since the book does not really address itself to the acts of all the apostles. After chapter one, very few of the twelve apostles are even mentioned by name. In studying Acts over the past several years, a number of more fitting titles have occurred to me. One of those might be "The Mistakes of Peter and Paul." The book gives us a detailed account of their many mistakes and causes us to wonder at the glory and the mystery of the church that has survived misguided, or mistaken leadership for so many years. Thank God for those times in history when leadership seemed to spring forth like a phoenix with dazzling brilliance. But there have been long periods of undistinguished leadership, and there may be more ahead. There is always a dearth of creative, courageous leadership but the church is still the church because it belongs to the Holy Spirit.

Another title I would suggest for Acts is "How the Good News Traveled from Jerusalem to Rome." When Jesus gave the commission "Go ye into all the world beginning in Jerusalem, Judea and Samaria and unto the uttermost parts," no place was farther from Jerusalem than Rome. The narrative ends in Rome. This is a story of how the Good News of the living God, raised from the dead and among us, was finally brought to the world center of that time—the capital of the Roman Empire.

The original Greek title for the Book of Acts is a very good one. It is simply "Acts of Apostolic People." That's far more to the point than "The Acts of the Apostles." This actually *is* an account of the acts of apostolic people, and that is crucial to our understanding of the church. The church is not an organization founded by Jesus during His earthly life and ministry. If that were so, then with His death, we would have become an historical society remembering how wonderful it was when God lived among us and spoke to us in the person of Jesus. With each generation we would have drifted farther away from our source.

In point of fact, we are still living the Book of Acts. The story of the acts of apostolic people continues as you and I are called to be apostolic people. This means we are as close to the Lord of the church as the twelve were in the first century. That's a mind-boggling concept and one that Luther emphasized. He said, "The church is not an organization with Jesus the founder. The church is an ecclesia, or a congregation, or a community of people as in the first century. It is a continuing community of people in whom the Lord is still alive and with whom the Lord is present."

To tell the story of the church, Luke begins with the fact that Jesus was raised from the dead. The resurrection is central to understanding the Good News. The Apostle Paul writes, "If Christ be not risen, we are of all people most miserable." This is the very foundation of the church. The Lord of the church is still living in and with and alongside His church. We are a community of people in whom He lives.

It seems to me there are only three views you can hold concerning the resurrection. First of all, you can say that those early apostles were mistaken. But the evidence for belief in the resurrection is not merely an empty tomb. The other evidence, which Luke reviews in the first chapter of Acts, is that Jesus was present for forty days. He built a bonfire, he cooked fish, he ate with the disciples and talked with them. You cannot be mistaken about someone alive and living with you for forty days whom you had previously seen buried. One important key to understanding the church comes to us in those beginning verses which emphasize that Jesus has been raised from the dead. There *was* a discontinuity, but *now* He is alive and with us.

Second, you can believe the resurrection story is a deliberate hoax. The disciples knew perfectly well that Jesus was not raised from the dead, but they perpetuated a fraud saying, "We know otherwise but we will conspire to spread this lie." I heard a talk by Charles Colson recently in which he reminded us that in the oval office, the most powerful place in the world, where the president reigns supreme, an attempted fraud and cover-up was exposed to the world in just six short weeks. With all the might of the nation at his disposal and with everything at stake, the president could not conceal his wrongdoing. How then, he conjectured, could a handful of poor, frightened, not too literate apostles live a lie all those years—years during which they were being persecuted, jailed, and even crucified? Unlikely, to say the least.

A third option, of course, is that the resurrection is true. It really happened. The most central fact in human history is that Jesus was raised from the dead, is alive, and is with us now. There is no other explanation for the behavior of the early Christians or that of Christians down through the ages in whom His Spirit lives.

In 1982, I was in Taiwan as a guest of that government. I had hoped while there to visit Mr. Kao, the general secretary of the Taiwanese Presbyterian church who is serving a seven-year term for his bold stance on civil liberty. I did not get to visit Mr. Kao but I did read a letter he had written to his denomination shortly after his imprisonment. In part it said, "Concerning the future of the church, I hope that you will very soon elect a new general secretary to assume the responsibility to support the church in evangelism and social responsibility. . . . A period of seven years will pass quickly. During this period I want to be trained to be a more faithful servant of Jesus Christ. When I am released, and if the churches still need me, I would like to be a traveling preacher. That is why I request that the church continue my status as a preacher, trusting that God will bless the whole church and all my fellow citizens." Only the fact of the resurrection explains this attitude of hope and trust in a man who is faced with seven years of imprisonment.

Art Beals, president of World Concern, wrote the following letter about one of our church missionaries, Colleen McGoff. "I remember seeing Colleen McGoff on a small, rocky island that serves as a refugee camp for Vietnamese people, the boat people, just off the coast of Malaysia. The day I saw her was the hottest, most uncomfortable day I've ever spent. Refugees were everywhere, and filth and frustration seemed to be the main ingredients of life in this boat-people camp. The sounds from the camp's loudspeakers were incessant, hour after hour calling out long lists of refugee names, announcing, instructing, warning, cajoling. How does anyone live in this mad atmosphere day after day? With a smile, Colleen told me that she wouldn't trade her work in these circumstances for any experience in life." Only the fact of the resurrection can account for Colleen and others like her who squander their lives in hopeless places and causes and count it all joy.

The birth of the church is described for us in the beginning of the second chapter of Acts. We read that "they were all together in one place [when] suddenly a sound from heaven came like the rush of a mighty wind, and it filled all the house where they were sitting. There appeared to them tongues as of fire, distributed and resting on each one of them. They were all filled with the Holy Spirit and began to speak in other tongues, as the Spirit gave them utterance" (vv. 2–4). Wind and fire—those were the manifestations when the Holy Spirit established the church. Jesus was raised from the dead and had ascended to heaven before the Holy Spirit came. God is One. He is a Father, He is Jesus the Son, and He is the Holy Spirit here and now. The Spirit called the church into being and gathered and empowered those frightened and discouraged apostles. The symbols or signs of His presence were a powerful wind, blowing through the Upper Room, and tongues as of fire over their heads.

I read about a trial in a Philadelphia court in which a fireman was suing the city. He had been fired because of his long hair. He was attempting to prove that his hair was not a fire hazard, but was, in fact, noncombustible. To demonstrate, he put a match to his hair and his whole head went up in flames. He was not seriously injured, and undaunted, he put the blame for this unexpected result on his hair spray. I don't know where the fire in the Upper Room came from and I don't know the source of the wind. Luke records that when the Spirit came it was *like* a mighty wind. It was *like* tongues of fire. Whether actual or symbolic, the point is wind and fire are two of the most terrifying and powerful forces in nature.

All through the Old Testament, God is associated with wind. We read of the *ruach* in the Old Testament or the *pneuma* in the New Testament, a Hebrew word and a Greek word describing kinds of wind. The wind is the sign of the invisible power of God. As for the fire, Moses was confronted by God in a burning bush.

The fire was the sign of God's presence. Fire out of control is terrifying. If you've witnessed a forest fire or watched a building burn, you are well aware of that. But a fire that is in control is both cheering and warming. Wind and fire, what appropriate symbols. Fire represents God's presence, and wind, His power. The Holy Spirit is the present tense of God, and these are the symbols of His presence and power in our lives. When we believe that God is truly present and when we appropriate His power, which is what Pentecost is all about, then we are an apostolic church. And that means that we continue to live out the Book of Acts—a book God is still writing—the acts of His apostolic people.

To be authentic apostolic people we must carry out a fourfold commission. First of all, we are evangelists. We are called to tell the Good News wherever we go. The Good News is not that all of us are rotten and sinful and need saving—though that's perfectly true. The Good News is that God knows our names and cares about us and thinks we're worth saving. There is an old rabbinical saying that "before every human being there goes a band of angels crying, 'Behold the image of God.'" We need to begin to believe that. Wherever we go, a band of angels is preceding us proclaiming that we are made in God's image. Our neighbors and friends need to know that. That's the heart of the whole message.

Second, apostolic people are involved in ministry. We are called to be ministers one to another. We're called to be those who love, affirm, heal, bless, and encourage one another in Jesus' name. When Jesus raised Lazarus from the grave, He turned to the surrounding company and commanded them to "loose him and let him go." Though now alive, he was bound up like a mummy for burial. We are still called to "unwrap" the Lazaruses among us and set one another free. We unbind one another. We call forth hidden gifts. When I was asked to give the commencement address at the Baylor School of Medicine Family Practice Division, I used that opportunity to tell them that 80 percent of their practice after graduation would not be biophysical. They would be treating the spiritual, emotional, and relational problems of mankind. I talked

about being healing people for each other, which is what apostolic people are called to be.

Third, apostolic people are on mission. We bring the good news from Jerusalem to Rome and we bring it to those at home as well. Last year our church received a call for help from a sister church less than two miles away. Their request was something like this: "We want to restructure our church. Our youngest member is over sixty. We live in a neighborhood full of young marrieds and singles. Will you send us a 'critical mass' of some of your best members, young and committed people? We want to evangelize the neighborhood." Our elders responded to that request and about thirty of our members have joined that church and begun an exciting new ministry there. The mission may be across the sea or only two miles away, but apostolic people are on mission.

Finally, apostolic people are involved in prophecy. Prophecy takes place when the people of God speak out about the evil and injustices and inadequacies of the structures and institutions of society. Prophecy means calling for new approaches to law or to health care or to government or penology or education.

In the next chapters we'll be doing a profile of the Holy Spirit and attempting to recapture His dream for His church. In redefining the church, I'm convinced we will find out who we are, a community of people in whom Jesus lives by His Holy Spirit, individuals commissioned to be evangelists, ministers, missionaries, and prophets. There is a place in the Amazon Basin, I am told, which has the richest resources of any place in the world and yet whose inhabitants are among the world's poorest. We Christians have the power and presence of the living God—His wind and fire. We need to continue to find a strategy to release that power and presence in and through us, that the church may be the church in our time.

CHAPTER ONE

God's Timing

ACTS 1:6–14

In 2 Chronicles 20:17, God tells Jehoshaphat, the military leader of the Israelites, who is surrounded by a great horde of enemy armies, "The word of the Lord comes to the armies of Israel. Stand still and see the salvation of your God." The message is to stand still and do nothing. The implication is that any effort to save yourself will prove to be counterproductive. God can sometimes demonstrate His power and presence best when we do nothing.

A few years ago I almost drowned in a storm at sea in the Gulf of Mexico when I found myself swimming far from shore, having tried to reach my drifting boat. I got into that predicament through my own stupidity, something not at all unusual. I can remember saying, "Well, this is it." The waves were seven or eight feet high, and the sky was dark with gale force winds and lightning. I was drifting out to sea when the Word of the Lord came to me and saved my life. What I thought He said was, "I'm here, Larson, and you're not coming home as soon as you think. Can you tread water?" Somehow that had never occurred to me. Had I continued my frantic efforts to swim back to shore, I would have exhausted my strength and gone down. In all sorts of situations we can make matters worse by our frantic efforts to save ourselves when God is trying to tell us, "Stand still." We have gotten ourselves into a hopeless situation and the more we do the worse it gets.

God gave quite the opposite instructions to the troops on the edge of the Promised Land. They had been wandering for forty years, during which time a whole generation died off and a new breed of young Israelites had come along to claim God's promise of a new land. He had prepared a place for them where He would be their God and they would be His people, and that transaction would be a blessing to millions in the years to come. In Joshua 1:3 we read, "Every place that the sole of your foot will tread upon I have given you." In other words, if you stand still you get nothing, but as you go out in faith claiming every place where you put your foot, it's all yours.

These conflicting messages present us with a dilemma. Just when do we stand still and when do we move out in faith and give the situation our best shot? It seems to me it's all a matter of timing. Timing is the key to spiritual power. The Bible speaks of two kinds of time, using the Greek words *chronos* and *kairos*. *Chronos* is the time we measure by hours, days, weeks, and years, with watches and calendars. That's one kind of time, and if we think we have only that dimension, we end up being what doctors call Type A personalities, driven workaholics prone to cardiovascular problems and heart attacks. Most of us are all too aware that we've got only so much measurable time, so we get up earlier and work longer and harder to accomplish all our goals. In the church we organize campaigns, plan revival services, and arrange stewardship drives. We work as if it all depended on us.

I believe God is trying to get through to us about another kind of time, not *chronos* but *kairos*. This Greek word translates as "in the fullness of time," or "the moment of opportunity." How much we need to recognize the *kairos* for our lives and for our time. When we do, the sale is made effortlessly; resources come together natu-rally; the right leadership team appears; communication opens up with that difficult person in your life. Perhaps you've been working hard at solving some problem in your business or in a relationship when, suddenly, a door opens and all you need do is walk through it and claim God's *kairos*.

In the first chapter of Acts the disciples are asking Jesus about the timing of the Kingdom. He answers, "It's not for you to know." He refuses to give us a timetable. I question anyone who claims to have a schedule for the last days. Just after this dialogue, the ascension takes place. After forty days of being with the disciples in His resurrection power, Our Lord physically leaves. The ascen-sion is difficult to explain in a Copernican universe where there is no "up." I'm convinced that Jesus disappeared dramatically into a cloud to demonstrate that the disciples would not see Him again physically. If He hadn't done this and they were to hear later on that He was in Italy or Greece, they'd assume He couldn't also be with them. So, as He makes His physical departure, He tells them to wait until He comes in spirit to be totally with them all the time. I believe the ascension was important as a demonstration that we will not see Him again until that eschatological moment when the whole world sees Him, when the play is over and the last curtain is drawn.

The disciples were instructed to go back to Jerusalem and wait for the *kairos*, that time when the church would be born and they would be able to move through the door God had already opened. Jesus operated on *kairos* time, not *chronos* time, as is powerfully demonstrated on the night of the Last Supper. He had come to the end of His ministry. He had trained twelve people. One would defect and the others were weak and wobbly. In this moment before going into His trial, His crucifixion, and all the horror of His last hours, what did He do? He threw a party. He arranged for a banquet, a leisurely meal—no fast food from a Jewish McDonald's or Colonel Sanders. Instead, He and His guests sat down probably to hors d'oeuvres, a main course, and even dessert. They sat around afterward and talked. Jesus in His most desperate hours was on *kairos* time. He said, "Come, we'll eat together and enjoy each other." He invites you to find the *kairos* for your life as well. If you're harried and frazzled, if you're a driven Type A—give it up. Come and enter into His *kairos* time and look for the moment of opportunity. Remember that verse that reminds us, "Again I saw that under the sun the race is not to the swift, nor the battle to the strong, nor bread to the wise, nor riches to the intelligent, nor favor to the men of skill; but time and chance happen to them all" (Eccles. 9:11).

This question the disciples posed before the ascension brings up another matter. Are we completing our agenda or working on God's? After forty days of fellowship with the risen Jesus, the disciples were thrilled. They had eaten together and fished together. We can imagine them thinking, "The resurrection was a pretty neat trick, Lord. But, now, putting that aside, let's get down to the real business [meaning *their* business]. Will you restore the Kingdom to Israel?" That never was Jesus' business. But they thought they could use Jesus as a means to their own ends.

To some extent we are all guilty of this, with God and with those around us. I'm often introduced to someone's fiancé(e) with words like "He/she is the answer to all my dreams." I say, "Yes, but are you the answer to his/her dreams?" So often we see the other person as a means of meeting our needs. We can have that attitude about our church. We join a church with all sorts of expectations. Here at last is an organization, a fellowship, who will help *me* do *my* thing, provide allies for my cause. The church is seen as a means to push *my* own projects and interests. The disciples were guilty of this, and we still do it. But rather than seeing Jesus as the means for accomplishing our agenda, we can say, "Lord, I want to belong to You. This is Your church and Your world. How can you put me on *Your* agenda for what You want to do in the world?"

It is this attitude that Paul expresses in Romans 8:28: "We know that in everything God works for good with those who love him, and who are called according to His purpose." Paul, who was shipwrecked, imprisoned, brought to trial, who narrowly escaped being lynched on a number of occasions, is nevertheless saying that all these things are working together for God's purposes. Since Paul is on God's agenda everything that happens is a step toward His end. This is the ultimate success story: if you're on God's agenda you can believe that everything that happens to you can have a purpose.

That was the experience of Henri Dunant, a wealthy Swiss banker of the last century. His government sent him to call on Napoleon in Paris in order to work out a mutually agreeable financial deal. He reached Paris only to learn that Napoleon was off doing battle with the Austrian army. Henri followed and arrived just in time to hear the trumpets blow and the battle begin. Cannons and muskets were exploding on every side. He watched cavalry charges and countercharges. He had a front seat for one of history's worst carnages and it affected him profoundly. When the battle subsided, Dunant stayed on to assist the doctors in treating the wounded in all the little farmhouses crammed with the dead and dying.

Eventually he went back to Switzerland, but he was never the same again. His experience left him with two obsessions: to abolish war and to help the suffering. He lost his fortune and eventually even his business, because banking no longer had his attention. But through his sole efforts, at the first Geneva conference the first international law was passed abolishing war. He was awarded the first Nobel Peace Prize, and though he was by that time penniless, he gave the prize money to advance his cause. He died in 1910, poor, unknown, and forgotten, but he left behind the Red Cross. Because of Henri Dunant, the Red Cross flag is the Swiss national flag in reversed colors, a white cross on a red shield. His dream was that this flag might be a symbol for all those who care about mercy in a suffering world. Dunant was God's instrument for calling the world to an antiwar movement and to a ministry of compassion—and it all came about because of his delayed appointment with Napoleon. On God's agenda everything that happens to us can have a purpose.

In Acts 1:8 we read, "You shall receive power and you will be My witnesses." The disciples were to act on the *kairos* principle.

After Jesus' ascension, they went back to the Upper Room where they had celebrated the Last Supper with Him and there they *waited*. They could accomplish nothing until the power came. When it came they began to move out and live dangerously; they became witnesses. It is significant that the word for witness in the Greek is the same one as the word for martyr. To be a witness you've got to be willing to be a martyr, which means that you put your life on the line. There is to be no frantic effort. When the *kairos* comes, you're on God's agenda; the door opens and you go through it and give it all you've got.

Some years ago I saw the National Football League championship game on TV. Dallas was playing Green Bay in Wisconsin, and it was really cold. They called that match the Ice Bowl. Green Bay was behind by five points, with just seconds left to play. Green Bay had the ball on the Dallas one-foot line and it was the fourth down and everything hinged on that last play. In that final huddle, we were told later, the quarterback, Bart Starr, turned to Jerry Kramer, the offensive guard, with this proposal: "Jerry, if you can move Jethro Pugh twelve inches to the left, you will make $15,000." Jerry was motivated enough to move Jethro, and Green Bay won the game. The point is, there are those times when we are to give extravagantly of ourselves, our substance, to lose our lives and give our all. And there are also those times when we are to wait for God's presence and power—His wind and fire.

The evangelization of Korea, sometimes called the most Christian nation in the world, is the product of *kairos*. The Christian missionaries did not arrive with the exploiters, the merchants and the military. Christian missions came to Korea with the liberators, and that flavor has lingered for almost two hundred years. Missionaries proclaimed, "If the Son shall set you free, you shall be free, indeed." The gospel in Korea is the gospel of liberation and it arrived in God's own *kairos*. How much all of us in the church need to wait for the *kairos*. The Kingdom will not come by more frantic effort and more doorbell ringing. It will come on God's agenda and it will come as we more and more make His agenda our own.

CHAPTER TWO

How the Holy Spirit Guides

ACTS 1:15–26

No matter how often some of us have studied the Book of
Acts, it is my hope that each time through we will find a
fresh perspective. We have been saying that if the church belongs
to the Holy Spirit, that person of the Trinity who is among us and
with us, then we have access to God in the same way that the first
century disciples did. How then do we understand His mind and
will? We are not some organization dedicated to perpetuating the
memory of Jesus. He is here among us. This is His church. The
beginning history of the church is *still* being written. It is
contemporary.

The chronicle begins, I believe, with an error of guidance.
Scholars are divided on this point. One of the great pulpit com-
mentators of all times, G. Campbell Morgan, says that the early
church began by electing the wrong person as the twelfth apostle,
since God had the Apostle Paul in mind all along. They cast lots

and chose Matthias, and that's the last we hear of him. Interestingly enough, they never cast lots again. Let's keep in mind they were operating on pre-Pentecostal guidance. In contrast to G. Campbell Morgan, F. F. Bruce, an eminent biblical scholar, insists they did the right thing. Matthias had all the requirements for apostleship. But whether you believe this selection was or was not a mistake, the Book of Acts records all sorts of mistakes made by the people of God in those early years. In this record, God's best plans and purposes are not always carried out. All of which brings up the whole question of guidance. If the church belongs to the Holy Spirit, how does the Spirit guide?

To begin with, I believe the Holy Spirit is certainly able to guide clearly. When He wants to get through to us individually or corporately, He will do so, make no mistake about it. When the time came for the church to break out of its Jewish ghetto and become a Gentile world faith, the Spirit spoke clearly to Cornelius, the Gentile, and Peter, the Jew. When Peter was imprisoned, the Holy Spirit woke him up and led him out. Phillip, in the midst of a revival in Samaria, was told to go down to a place in the desert. There he met the Ethiopian eunuch and thence the gospel moved into another culture and region. Paul received his Macedonian vision to take the Gospel to a whole new continent. Indeed, the Book of Acts indicates that when the Spirit wants to communicate explicit guidance, there is no problem. He can speak clearly and precisely.

I think most of us have experienced, in at least one place in our lives, God's clear and unmistakable will for us. We have prayed and asked for specific directions and known with certainty what He meant for us to do. We have abundant proof that God is able to tell us something if He wants to.

But does the Holy Spirit *always* guide clearly? The obvious answer from the Book of Acts is no. Think again, objectively, of some watershed time in your life when you received no direction, even after long and agonized prayer and perhaps even fasting. Those times confirm that the Holy Spirit does not *always* guide us, even though we know He can.

The Scriptures are not a guidebook on how to live our lives

without making mistakes, though some seem to think they are. They believe that if we really understood the Bible, we would have clear direction at every point in our lives. It seems to me, however, that the Book of Acts particularly is a record of how God allows us to make mistakes and how He can redeem those mistakes and even help us to change. As we read the Book of Acts, we can see that the behavior of the apostles seems to change. At one point they react to a certain situation in a particular way, and a few chapters later, they handle the same situation differently. The Book of Acts, then, is not a guidebook for leading an infallible "Christian" life. Rather, it is a source of encouragement that, while God allows us to make mistakes, for some reason known to Him, He can redeem those mistakes and even put them to creative use.

The truth is that we already know God's will in almost every major daily decision we face. Asking for guidance can easily be a cop-out. We often procrastinate by saying, "God, tell me clearly what to do and I'll do it." When God spoke through Ezekiel to the spiritual leaders of Israel, He condemned them for fattening themselves and their families and for hankering after riches when they had been entrusted with the care of God's family. They were scourged for not doing that which He had clearly told them to do. They didn't need guidance in terms of God's will. They needed a prophet among them to convict them and bring them to repentance and a change of heart.

Think of some big decision you've had to make in the last month—financial, vocational, moral, or ethical. Suppose I asked you (assuming you are not an orphan) what advice your parents would have given you in that situation. You might not agree with the course of action they would have proposed, but I'll bet you know exactly what advice they'd have given. You know because you are aware of their values. You've lived with them, watched them, eaten at their table, received their love. Whether you have accepted or rejected those values, you've absorbed them. Similarly, if you are God's person and you have lived with Him, worshiped Him, served Him, and read His word, you have a pretty clear idea of what He expects of you. You can get about doing it without waiting for guidance.

I am on the board for the Christian Conciliation Service of Puget Sound, a new ministry dedicated to helping people resolve legal disputes without litigation. Many of our members serve as conciliators on panels set up to mediate disputes over divorce settlements, child custody, and financial liability of all kinds. At some point, a conciliator may say to one of the parties, "Yes, you've got a case. This person has wronged you, but have you considered forgiveness?" We are discovering that most professing Christians have never even considered forgiveness as a remedy for a life situation. Every Sunday, if not daily, most Christians repeat the prayer, "Forgive us our debts as we forgive our debtors." But we never apply that in terms of a legal dispute. We are told clearly to love one another as Jesus has loved us; we don't need to ask for guidance in this matter of forgiveness.

In the winter of 1982 in the midst of a national economic crunch, Mayor Koch of New York made an appeal to the churches of the city. There were no public funds to help at least thirty-six thousand homeless men and women who were facing a terrible winter, and Koch suggested that the thirty-five hundred churches in Manhattan might undertake their care, which would mean about ten persons per congregation, Catholic, Jewish and Protestant. Those families would receive better care and at no public expense. The churches responded with a great silence. When the *New York Times* investigated the story, they quoted one Protestant minister who said, "The mayor never mentioned this to me. Nobody in his office apprised me of this." The Catholic spokesman sidestepped the question, and a leading Jewish rabbi said, "We haven't money to heat the building for this extra service." Of course the *Times*'s reaction to these responses was scathing. Jesus' instructions are clear in Matthew 25:35: "I was a stranger and you took me in. . . ." All too often our reply is, "Lord, you didn't give us time to analyze the proposal." We need not wait for guidance to begin to care for the poor. That is an explicit part of God's general will for all of us.

It seems to me there is something wrong with wanting God's clear, indisputable guidance at every turn. As for me, that feeds my inordinate need for a life of safety and certainty. If God sends me a clear message, which He does sometimes, then I can say, "I'll do it, win or lose. I'm doing God's will." There is no risk involved. But God wants a relationship with us more than He wants infallibility. He wants us to learn to trust Him. I'm convinced that that is why He sometimes withholds His guidance. He is saying, "You know what to do. Move in the right direction. I want you to trust me." Our witness to the world is that we can move out in faith trusting a God who is with us in every situation.

One of my favorite theater moments comes in *Fiddler on the Roof* when Tevye, the old husband, turns to his wife of many, many years, and asks, "Do you love me?" Her reply is to list all she has done for him—cooking, washing, cleaning, raising his children. Obstinately he persists, "But do you love me?" He doesn't want just a faithful, dutiful, obedient wife. He wants a lover. I think God wants more than a faithful, dutiful, infallible servant. He wants us to love and trust Him. He wants us to move out into the unknown, to be unafraid because we love Him. That kind of trust is better than positive guidance.

Insisting on definite and specific guidance at every step is a way of avoiding responsibility. If I know it's God's will, how can I fail? If it's not God's will, I may fail, but what's wrong with failing? The cross is the means by which God forgives our failures. If we don't accept that forgiveness, we become very cautious people, afraid to take risks. If we are afraid to fail, we haven't grasped the reality of the grace of God. He urges us to move out in faith and it's OK to fail.

Sometimes we insist on certain and clear guidance because of our need to feel superior. Many of us have a great need to say to another, "God told me what you should do, so shape up." I don't think God operates that way. I'm even wary of the TV evangelist who told his audience recently that a vision of Jesus appeared to him with the message that they should support a particular cause he was promoting. Frankly, I have a hard time with those who claim they have a direct pipeline to God and can therefore tell the rest of us what to do and be. I recently heard a preacher say that there are no heroes in the Bible except God. I believe that, but I still want to be a hero, somebody who has a little edge on the rest of you. I'd like to be someone who can tell you absolutely what God's will is, but I just don't think God works that way.

How can we legitimately expect the Holy Spirit to guide? Do we cast lots as the apostles did? Do we take a lucky dip in the Bible and find just the right verse? Do we follow our hunches? Do we have a quiet time of prayer and meditation and write down any thoughts that come? Well, some of those methods may work at certain times. I think we can try all of them in the firm belief that God does want to guide us very clearly at those forks in the road when much is at stake.

Certainly He guides us through prayer. Prayer is dialogue. We tell God about our hurts and we intercede for others, but half of our prayer time ought to be spent in listening as the other partner in the dialogue speaks to us.

God can guide through the Bible. The Bible is the consistent source for understanding God and His general will for us.

There are times when we are guided in community, the fellowship of believers. God has promised to be with us where two or three are gathered to pray, to read the Scriptures, to be on mission together. God's Spirit is present in a group like that even more than in those times of solitary communion. I have found this to be especially true in these past few years in the pastorate. I am moderator of our church's session, which, in the Presbyterian system, is our ruling body of elders. There have been times when I disagreed with the majority vote and said so, only to admit later that in God's overall purposes it was the right vote. In submitting to the will of the group, even when I think they're wrong, I am trusting God with the whole-group process.

But, finally, having received guidance through any of these means—prayer, listening, reading the Bible, through the prayers of a group of believers—we must act on it, throw our lives into it. We are to do this even though that course seems uncertain and fraught with disaster. Things may go wrong. There are dangers and risks in this kind of living, but that's where we begin to trust God, and trusting Him is more important than being right or guided.

When we received the call to our present parish in Seattle, we tried very hard to find God's clear guidance. We prayed and read the Bible and talked to our most immediate small group—our three children. Two of them advised against the move, while one said it sounded like God's will. We talked by phone to three of our oldest and dearest friends. Two thought it sounded like the right move, and one cautioned against it. All of this checking around produced three affirmatives and three negatives. I said, "Lord, thanks a bunch. You know we want to do your will. What is it?"

At that point the Lord seemed to get through clearly. I felt He was saying something like this: "Suppose you go there and it isn't my will and the whole thing falls apart (which is precisely what I was afraid of)? So what? You've failed before and I'll be in the failure and we can make compost out of it. It's a thriving church and it will survive having the wrong pastor for a few years. On the other hand, suppose I want you there and suppose that because you're not certain and don't trust me, you don't go. You'll blow a great opportunity to serve." In that spirit, we said "yes" and returned to the parish ministry. We are still there and are still saying occasionally, "Is this the right place, Lord?"

G. K. Chesterton, one of my favorite writers, once said, "If a thing is worth doing, it's worth doing poorly." If it's worth doing, you can't afford to wait until you have all your ducks lined up. If it's worth doing, do it even if failure seems inevitable. Throw your life into it. That's the only way to respond to God's eternal question, "Do you trust me? Do you trust me?"

CHAPTER THREE

The Problem with Pentecost

ACTS 2:1–21

The miracle of the church is that it defies all human
manipulation. There is no way to account for the survival and growth of the church, apart from the fact that the Holy
Spirit Himself has called us into being and continues to empower
and control us. William Temple, the great ecumenical archbishop of England during the early part of this century, has said,
"The supreme wonder of the history of the Christian church is that
always, in the moments when it has seemed most dead, out of its
own body there has sprung up new life." That has been true since
the church's beginning days. After Jesus' death and resurrection,
eleven apostles were left. They were frightened men, not academi-
cians, not worldly wise by most standards; yet God used those
eleven out of all proportion to their abilities. In his first sermon
Peter stood and addressed thousands with dignity, brilliance, and
boldness. This kind of life-changing miracle happens over and
over again in the history of the church.

You may recall the dramatic time in English history when King Henry II contrived to make his friend Thomas à Becket Archbishop of Canterbury in order to control all branches of power. But as soon as Becket was invested as archbishop, something happened to him. He took his office seriously and defied his sovereign, to the king's surprise and outrage. That's not an isolated instance. Often some mysterious work of the Spirit takes place in the lives of those unexpectedly called to positions of power in the church as pastors, elders, deacons, and teachers. There is no way to account for the church, apart from the Spirit's calling forth leadership.

The events of Pentecost are a fulfillment of many Old Testament promises. We find in Isaiah 32:15 the wistful prophecy, "Until the Spirit is poured upon us from on high, and the wilderness becomes a fruitful field. . . ." Isaiah is longing for this indwelling that will someday happen. In his sermon, Peter wants his hearers to understand that these events of Pentecost were no accident. God planned it all. He reminds them that the prophet Joel said, "And in the last days it shall be, God declares, that I will pour out my Spirit upon all flesh, and your sons and your daughters shall prophesy, and your young men shall see visions, and your old men shall dream dreams" (Acts 2:17, RSV).

In those days Pentecost was a traditional Jewish harvest festival, the Feast of Weeks. It came fifty days after Passover, and Jews came to Jerusalem from all the surrounding countryside for this very traditional festival. God chose this Pentecost time to fulfill His prophecy. It was while all these visitors were in the city that, for the first time, He poured out His Holy Spirit on all believers.

We have heard a great deal about the Holy Spirit in the past twenty or thirty years, thanks to the charismatic Christians among us. I am grateful for them because they have reminded us that every believer is a receiver of the Holy Spirit. They have helped us focus on the work of the Spirit and the gifts of the Spirit. In one sense, we are all charismatic Christians. It is only by the work of the Spirit that we become believers.

If you are a believer, you experience Pentecost at the time of your conversion. Whatever your background, at one point you have said to yourself (and these feelings may have been building for days, weeks, months, or years), "I am unhappy with my life." Like the Apostle Paul, you say, "'That which I would not, that I do, and that which I would, I do not.' I keep making a mess of my life. I am guilty of failing the people I love the most." You are overwhelmed with despair. That conviction of sin is the gift of the Holy Spirit. Until that time, you were blaming other people for your problems: your parents, friends, your spouse, your kids or your co-workers. The Spirit is at work in your life when you take responsibility for your predicament.

But the work of the Spirit is twofold. Aside from pointing out our sinfulness, the Spirit points us to Jesus, who cares, who has redeemed us, who says, "All is forgiven. Come home. I want to live my life in you." Your personal Pentecost happens when these two experiences come together. You understand your own sinfulness, but you have hope because you enter a new relationship with God. That cannot take place apart from the work of the Holy Spirit.

In the nineteenth chapter of Acts, Paul asks the new converts at Ephesus if they have received the Holy Spirit since they believed. They reply that they haven't even heard of the Holy Spirit. They had been baptized into John's baptism (a baptism marking repentance from sin). Paul tells them about Jesus and they receive the Holy Spirit. The new baptism centers in the person of Jesus; when we understand who He is and confess our sins and our needs, something new happens.

One of the leaders in the charismatic movement in the past thirty or forty years has been David du Plessis. His own background is charismatic and Pentecostal, but his ministry has been to the church at large. He has been reminding us that the Holy Spirit is central to our life in the church. I have often heard him say something like this: "The church has been a repository for two thousand years of the most incredible truth in the world, truth about man's need and God's love and grace. The church has kept this truth in the deep-freeze as you would a steak. Now if you offer that frozen steak to a hungry person, it's of no practical use to him or her. But if you put that steak on the grill with a fire under it, suddenly the fat starts to sizzle, the juices begin to run, and you begin to smell the aroma of roasting meat. That steak becomes negotiable to the hungry party. The Holy Spirit is the vehicle by which the fire is lit under old truths so that even nonbelievers are attracted." I really enjoy that interpretation of the Holy Spirit. We've all been to churches where the gospel is being preached but there is no aroma, or at least no pleasant one.

At Pentecost we discover a new person in the Trinity. God is the Father and Creator. In Jesus He is the Son and Redeemer and, beginning with Pentecost, we know Him as the Holy Spirit. One God, but three persons—the great mystery. Who is the Holy Spirit? He is God, as is Jesus, as is the Father and Creator. The Holy Spirit is a person, not a doctrine or a force. He comes to dwell in you and me by God's promise and grace, and when we leave worship on Sunday, it is that Third Person in the Trinity who goes with us to our homes, our schools, our offices and factories.

On the day of Pentecost, a whole new avenue of communication opened up. What happened is in direct contrast to the Old Testament story of the Tower of Babel. That was the account in which men wise in their own conceits decided to join forces to erect a great tower. However, they had such language barriers that they could not communicate and total chaos erupted. This is a continuing problem. Relationships deteriorate because we are unable to hear what the other person is saying. We don't hear the "I love you's" or "Help me's" or "I need you's" and we become defensive, blind, and deaf at the emotional level.

So often we hear what we expect to hear, rather than what is said. I heard about a little girl who was singing, "Sing a song of six packs, a pocket full of rye. . . ." I'm sure she never heard of sixpence, while six packs are all too familiar. When I was a student at Princeton Seminary, the famous Robert Oppenheimer, the scientific genius behind the atomic bomb, was teaching a graduate course at the University. I decided to attend and somehow managed to slip unnoticed into a class on thermodynamics. I chose a seat in the back row, lest I be called on, and I was there for an hour.

Oppenheimer's first two words were, "Good morning," and those were the last two words I fully understood. He wrote some material on the blackboard and students were taking notes, but it was all in a language unknown to me. I'm as lost when someone tries to talk to me about computers. They are totally baffling.

Nobody could miss what happened at Pentecost. Everybody who was there understood in his or her own language. Even those who were visitors from all sorts of far-off places. In the description of the crowd, it is said that almost all the nations of the known world at that time in history are listed. Symbolically, every known language was heard and was understood. It was the very opposite of the confusion of tongues of the Tower of Babel. There was direct, clear communication which we can't quite explain.

Henry Pitney Van Dusen, a former president of Union Seminary in New York, wrote a perceptive book called *Spirit, Son and Father.* He said the church today, in presenting the doctrine of the Trinity, has reversed the order of the three Persons of the Godhead. We speak of Father, Son, and Spirit. The Father is the member of the Trinity we present to the world. We talk about Jesus to the inner group of believers, and the concept of the Holy Spirit is reserved for the spiritually mature. Van Dusen insisted that the Spirit is the most negotiable and discernible person in the Trinity. You can walk into a church in which the Holy Spirit is present and smell the sizzle that du Plessis speaks about. You feel loved, cared for, and accepted. Anybody can discern whether or not the Spirit is present in a gathering. According to Van Dusen, understanding Jesus is more difficult, while understanding God the Father is most difficult of all. But the Spirit is the one who communicates His presence and produces life and hope. He is here, or He is not here. His presence is always discernible.

The Spirit gives us new gifts for ministry. But even better than the gifts are the fruits of the Holy Spirit. Paul listed them in his letter to the Galatians. They are love, joy, peace, patience, kindness, goodness, faithfulness, gentleness, and self-control. The gifts of the Spirit can be counterfeited, but only God can give us the fruits of the Spirit. When we are around someone filled with love and joy and peace and all those other qualities, the aroma is overpowering. Their authenticity is incontrovertible.

The ultimate gift of the Spirit at Pentecost is the church itself. As we said earlier, the church was born at Pentecost when the Spirit gave us to one another. Some of Jesus' last words to Peter were about ministry within the church. Peter had been following Jesus for three years, healing the sick, casting out demons and proclaiming the Kingdom of God. But by contrast with the next task, that was easy stuff. In fact, Peter could not have accomplished the next task until a new spirit came upon him. When Peter had been converted, or changed, or filled with the Holy Spirit at Pentecost, then he was to strengthen the brethren.

The hardest job of all is to love the people in the household of God. It's much easier to seek out some stranger in the street, to find some poor soul in need and take him home for a night or two, or give him some money, or pray with him. But how about that person who has been sitting in the pew next to you or in front of you for the last thirty years, with whom you seem always to be at cross-purposes? To love one another can be the hardest task of all. When we in the church can do that, the world will beat down our doors. There is a universal hunger for a fellowship like that. The church was born at Pentecost, and the power released then enables us to embrace not only the world out there but one another, and to help each other become all God meant us to be.

I heard a moving story from a pastor friend of mine in New England. One of his church's missionaries is Ruth Seabury, who works in India. She reported a conversation she had had with one of the great Hindu social workers. At one point, he asked her, "Do you think most Christians know what they've got?" Perplexed by the question, she asked what he had in mind. He said, "Every religion has a god. Every religion has an altar. Every religion has worshipers. Every religion believes in sacrifice. But only Christians have a Saviour and only Christians have a congregation." A congregation is not just an audience of people sitting in neat rows, listening, worshiping, giving. It's a group made one in the Spirit, and in that group resides the power of God to heal, to bless, to liberate, to transform. As a congregation, we are not supporters of some particular philosophy. We are a holy family in which the power of God resides.

What, then, is the problem with Pentecost? The problem is not the wind that seemed to fill the room, as if it were a mighty wind. Wind has always been associated with God, as we said earlier. We read in Ezekiel about the Valley of Dry Bones. He says, "Lord, will these bones live?" You and I have been dry bones. We have been without hope, and God sends His Spirit over those dry bones. As the wind of God blows, the dry bones come together and we are alive.

There is no problem with the fire. Fire is a symbol of God because it purifies and consumes, it cheers, it warms. There were tongues *as* of fire. God appeared to Moses in the burning bush. John the Baptist said that while he baptized with water, One would be coming after him who would baptize with the Holy Spirit and with fire. Fire has always been a sign of God's consuming, awesome presence. The Protestant reformer John Calvin, a man of passion, chose as his crest an upraised hand holding a burning heart. Beneath that crest are inscribed these words, "Lord, my heart I give Thee, eagerly and sincerely." The heart set aflame by God was Calvin's crest. That's the gift of Pentecost to you and to me—a heart on fire. That fire burns and is not consumed.

There is no problem with the tongues. We don't quite know what happened. Later in the New Testament, we find that tongues required an interpreter, and they still do. But in this first manifestation, no interpretation was required.

The real problem comes because the Spirit was poured out on all. In the Old Testament, the Spirit was given only to the selected few. Those special prophets and judges and kings spoke for God to the Israelites, who then had the choice of believing them or not. In the new covenant that God began at Pentecost, all of us who are believers are called to be priests and prophets. Everybody has direct access to the Chairman of the Board at all times, whether we use that privilege or not. We can knock on His door morning, noon, or night. We can commune with the Holy Spirit, and we can prophesy if we want to. Now that causes an enormous problem in church government. How do you govern a church full of chiefs?

A friend of mine who lives near Hoyt Park in Madison, Wisconsin happens to be a great bird lover. Invariably, his yard is full of all kinds of birds in all seasons. However, the squirrels plague his bird feeders continually. Exasperated, he finally bought a pellet gun and began to shoot squirrels, two and three a day, every day, week after week. In spite of these desperate measures, the squirrel population seemed undiminished. One day, he was discussing this irksome problem with his colleague at work. His friend said, "I solved that problem. I was troubled by squirrels too. But now I trap them. I trap two or three a day and take them down to Hoyt Park and release them." That's an example of what can happen when we approach all of our problems individually, with no sense of the larger picture.

Pentecost presents us with this kind of problem, and it's for the most part a great kind of problem to have. Our church in Seattle is full of chiefs. The youngest, the newest, the greenest of us has total access to the Chairman of the Board. An authentic New Testament church must learn how to operate with a church full of chiefs. No one pastor or one staff or one board is in charge. Rather, we somehow harness the resources that are ours corporately. We are together able to be God's people with access to Him. That requires taking time every day to listen to Him. When we listen to what the Spirit is saying to us, we have wisdom and courage. We have boldness and we have comfort. All those are available because of the one who dwells in us.

Calvin Coolidge was once asked, "Who lives in the White House?" He said, "Nobody. They keep coming and going." The miracle of the church is that it is inhabited by the Holy Spirit—not the building, but the living stones, you and me. We are the church and we have access to God at all times. That's the miracle that began at Pentecost.

CHAPTER FOUR

The View from the Pew

ACTS 2:22–40

One of the vital ingredients of the New Testament church was good preaching. That's still an important component of our corporate church life, and in this chapter we will look closely at the first Christian sermon ever preached—Peter's sermon at Pentecost. Preaching may seem to many an anachronistic art form; yet, there is nothing quite like a good sermon. Unlike books, plays or newspapers, a sermon is a unique means of communicating God's Good News.

I was away from the pastorate for twenty-one years, years spent as an itinerant evangelist in a faith mission. But when I wasn't traveling, I enjoyed the view from the pew. I would attend my home church regularly, always with great expectations. Even now when I am in my own pulpit on most Sundays, I look forward to those vacation opportunities to visit local churches, wherever we are, hoping to find preaching that will thrill my soul and change my life. I have about a half-dozen preacher friends around the country who send me their printed sermons. I read them on my day off, and they bless me. I like to think I am a connoisseur of sermons and I thank God that He has ordained the foolishness of preaching as a means of revealing His truth to us.

Consider the many times in the history of spiritual awakening and renewal that have been associated with the names of great preachers. There was John Wesley in eighteenth century England and in the mid-nineteenth century, there was Charles Finney, the renowned lawyer-turned-preacher. We think of Jonathan Edwards and the Great Awakening in New England, or Dwight Moody, the uneducated layman who became one of the great popular preachers of all time. Farther back, we find preachers like Saint Ignatius of Loyola or Saint Francis of Assisi, who brought the gospel to slaves, pirates and lepers, as well as to kings and princes.

About one hundred and twenty-five years ago, the French government sent the famous sociologist and historian Alexis de Tocqueville to study America and to write an unbiased report on just what makes America so great. He spent several years here, talking to all kinds of people, including leaders in government, business, and the professions. His assay of America filled a great volume, but the conclusion was summed up in this way: "I sought for the greatness and genius of America in her commodious harbors and ample rivers and it was not there. I sought for the greatness and genius of America in her fertile fields and boundless forests, and it was not there. I sought for the greatness and genius of America in the public school system and her institutions of learning and it was not there. Not until I went into the churches of America and heard her pulpits flame with righteousness, did I understand the secret of her genius and her power." That statement reflects the profound role played by the pulpit message in preserving and continuing the rich heritage received from those who came here with the single desire to worship God in freedom.

What is a good sermon? What do we have a right to expect as God's faithful people occupying the pews? How does Peter's Pentecost sermon help us here?

Let's start with some of the things a good sermon is not. First of all, it is not spiritual entertainment. I have heard many sermons that were biblical, interesting, humorous and neatly packaged in a twenty-minute frame, but had no message. They simply filled the time pleasantly with truths about God. Preaching is not like teaching. It is not like witnessing, though we are called to be witnesses wherever we go to what Jesus Christ has done in our lives. It's not prophecy, though we are called at times to be prophets, and to speak forth for God. Preaching is none of those things.

Preaching is not meant to be guilt-reducing. A preacher is not to be a "Doctor Feel-Good." That's a term for those doctors who are dedicated not to healing but to making us feel better, who pop their patients full of painkillers and tranquillizers in their concern to numb our discomfort and insure our good will. Well, there are feel-good preachers as well. The message is a familiar one— "What does it matter? Nobody's perfect. We're all going the same way. We all make mistakes. All roads lead to the same end." That is *not* the biblical message. Authentic preaching presents law and judgment as well as grace. A few years ago psychiatrist Karl Menninger wrote a book called *Whatever Became of Sin?* A good sermon has to deal realistically with the fact that you and I, basically, are rebellious, stubborn people whom God loves. Sin must be dealt with in the light of God's grace.

Since Peter's day, sermons may have changed in style somewhat because the times have changed, but the message is the same. As we read Peter's words from that first day when the church was born and the Holy Spirit given, we have before us a model of what a good sermon is.

First of all, a sermon ought to be personal and immediate. It needs to be both specific and incarnational. The foolishness of preaching is that God chooses a spokesman or spokeswoman in a particular time and place to talk to a particular people. The sermon that floats along on generalities and that could be preached at any time in any age has no immediacy for its hearers. A good sermon is, first of all, inspired by God and then delivered by a particular person to a specific audience.

One great definition of a sermon was given by Phillips Brooks in a Yale lecture series years ago. He said, "Preaching is God's truth revealed through personality." In other words, if you take away the personality, you don't have a sermon; at best you have some sort of disconnected truth indicating that "God is." A good sermon ought to reveal something of the nature of the preacher, of the setting in which it was preached and of the people to whom it was preached.

We went to Taiwan with a cultural delegation as guests of the Taiwanese government. Since we were there over a Sunday, my wife and I with three other delegates went to a local church. Shortly after the service began, the preacher said, "I see we have a preacher from the States in the congregation. I'm going to ask Bruce Larson to come up here and give the message this morning." I experienced sheer terror, since I had no message from the Lord for that occasion. Beyond that, I knew nothing about the congregation except that about half were Taiwanese and the other half were European or American. The only people I knew anything about were my four traveling companions. So I stood up and prayed hard and preached a sermon I thought might speak to those four people.

Peter's preaching is personal. He began with himself and moved on to include his audience. In essence, he was saying, "I am one of the twelve, and I know who you are and what your history is. Let me tell you about it."

A good sermon needs to be relevant. It must answer the questions that are being asked. Too many sermons provide answers to unasked questions. The people Peter was addressing were asking questions. "What does this mean? Why are you speaking in a strange language? We thought Jesus was dead. Please explain all this." Peter talked about the resurrection. He answered their questions.

A good sermon has a clear purpose. When I have the opportunity to talk to young ministers about preaching, I offer this suggestion: "Before you begin to write any sermon ever, write your purpose in one sentence at the top of the page. What is it you hope God will do in the hearts of those who hear this message? What

specific, concrete thing are you hoping God will accomplish because you have taken twenty or twenty-five minutes of the congregation's time? If you have that clearly in mind, everything you
write builds to that purpose." Peter must have had a clear purpose
in mind, because when his sermon ended, his hearers said, "What
can we do?" He was ready with a plan of action for them. They
heard the message that something was required of them. Peter told
them to repent and be baptized; that's what they were to do.

A good sermon is biblical, grounded in Scripture. I am wary of
sermons that are not expository. The Bible deals with every possible human situation—relational, political, or social. It's all there.
Scripture is powerful. As I said, for twenty-one years I have been
enjoying the view from the pew. Over those years, even when the
preacher seemed dull or irrelevant, if he suddenly quoted three or
four verses of Scripture, life somehow broke through. There is
power in the word of God. We experience that power as we preach
from it, quote it, and store it in our hearts. In his sermon Peter
quoted freely from the Old Testament as he talked about the Good
News.

But while a good sermon is scriptural, it is not *about* the Bible. It
points to Jesus. That's the kerygma—the proclamation. The Bible
is God's word, but that word points to God among us in Jesus
Christ. We don't preach the Bible; we preach Jesus. In the fifth
chapter of John's Gospel, Jesus said to the leaders of the synagogue, "You search the scriptures, because you think that in
them you have eternal life; and it is they that bear witness to me; yet
you refuse to come to me that you may have life" (John 5:39–40).
In preaching we are to use the word of God with great diligence,
but that word points to the living Word who is among us.

Someone has said there are three kinds of sermons. We can
preach about *him* or *her* or *it*. A sermon about *him* is about Jesus,
about God the Father, Son, and Holy Spirit. A sermon about *her* is
about the church. The *it* is Christianity, Christian ethics and
behavior. Authentic sermons are sermons about the Lord of the
church. We read of the Greeks who came to the disciples asking,
"Sir, we would see Jesus." I've seen those words in hundreds of

pulpits I've occupied around the country, posted so that only the preacher can see them. It is a mandate from the faithful people of God. They have a right to see Jesus, the center of the Good News.

A good sermon uses lots of stories. That was Jesus' own method. Stories are the windows through which we glimpse truth. After endless words and erudite phrases, the preacher says, "That reminds me of something that happened this week—" Or, "I saw a man yesterday who—" Our attention is caught, and suddenly a window is opened and light comes in. Jesus was always telling stories. "A man was sowing seed. . . . A woman lost a coin. . . . A certain man had two sons. . . ." Right away we have a mental picture. Paul told his own story frequently. Just as the mob is about to kill him, he says, "Wait a minute. A funny thing happened to me on the way to Damascus," and he proceeds to tell his conversion story.

A good sermon is interesting. The ultimate heresy is to make the gospel boring. We Christians have the greatest news in the world, powerful news. Anyone who is making that dull has a right to hear from those of us in the pews. A good sermon is touched with humor. Elton Trueblood has written a book about the humor of Jesus. He was not grim. He wept at funerals, but he was able to laugh.

I love Peter's response when the disciples are accused of being drunk. He does not give some pious reply, such as, "We are temperance people. How dare you accuse us of drinking?" His reply is one of the great one-liners of the New Testament. He says, "It's only the ninth hour." In other words, it's too early to be drunk. He parries their attack with something whimsical.

A good sermon implies that the preacher is under judgment too. Preachers get their authority from the fact that God has called them to preach, not from their perfection. On Sunday morning, I have a mandate to tell my congregation what I think God is saying to us about how to live this day, this week in our hometown, as His people. When I leave the pulpit, I may say to one of my hearers, "What in the world did I say? How do we do that? Help me." Together we have access to the Holy Spirit who will give us wisdom and who will guide us. Every preacher is under judgment. The message from the pulpit falls upon us preachers as well as upon our congregations.

I was reading recently about Ken Strachen, the founder of Latin American Mission, one of the most effective evangelical missions in the world. Elisabeth Elliot wrote *Who Shall Ascend*, a biography on Strachen in which she said that this creative, bold missionary, who inspired so many, is revealed in his own prayer journals as a man full of doubts. The journals reflect his continual questions about his ministry and his ability to carry it out. Who is the real Ken Strachen? The one who led a powerful mission or the frail human being, struggling with his own identity, his own worth, and his own salvation in the Lord? Certainly he is both, as you and I are both. All authentic preachers have the same struggle.

Finally, a good sermon must offer hope. When the crowd asked Peter what they must do, he said, "Repent and be baptized for the remission of sins, *for the promise is to you and to your children.*" When we become believers, all those in our household are blessed by our faith and our prayers. Our children are part of the covenant until they come of age and make vows for themselves. The news that we proclaim, that you and I live out, is Good News. A good sermon emphasizes this hopeful news. It may spell out our disobedience, our sins, our doubts, but it reminds us we needn't stay like that. This week things can be different.

A good sermon is judged in the final analysis by its effectiveness. After this particular sermon of Peter's, three thousand people found the Lord. Not a bad sermon!

CHAPTER FIVE

Let the Church Be the Church

ACTS 2:41–47

When I was at Princeton Seminary, our president was Dr. John Mackay, former Scottish missionary to South America and one of the Lord's luminous old saints. He never spoke in a chapel service—or anyplace else for that matter—that he did not use the phrase "Let the church be the church." In other words, the church can be like no other institution. His plea was that the church be nothing more nor less than the church.

Helmut Thielicke, a well-known German Lutheran pastor who was imprisoned during Hitler's time, prolific writer and statesman, has said that "The church cannot permit its authority to be defined by people who have no idea of its mission." The church must not be shaped by society or any other force, but by the Lord of the church Himself.

Sometimes the church aspires to be something else in the interest of progress. But progress is sometimes made at the expense of basics. The well-known columnist James Reston, one of our premier journalists, quotes his ninety-four-year-old Presbyterian mother as saying, "All this progress is merely wickedness going faster." We do need to examine whatever progress we make as the church in society and be certain we are not losing our basics.

In a speech to the General Assembly of the Presbyterian Church, Dr. Richard Halverson, chaplain to the U.S. Senate, was challenging the church to come back to its roots. He said, "In the beginning the church was a fellowship of men and women centering on the living Christ. Then the church moved to Greece, where it became a philosophy. Then it moved to Rome, where it became an institution. Next it moved to Europe where it became a culture, and, finally, it moved to America where it became an enterprise." He was reminding us that every culture tends to corrupt its institutions.

We in the church must continually reemphasize the fact that we belong to the Lord of the church and ask Him what it is He would have us be. It seems to me that we have a tendency toward what I call ecclesiastical anthropomorphism, which means that we project on the church whatever we need it to be. We make the church over in our own image.

We use the church to push our causes or to promote our chosen life style. It's interesting to think about the church of the eighteenth century in merry old England. It was a merry old church. Some believers broke away and came to New England with their Puritan ethics and austere life styles. They were for the most part dour and unhappy, suspicious of anyone having a good time. I'm sure both branches of the church, the New World settlers and those who stayed at home, considered their life style the authentic one.

Or, we find that the church becomes a haven for our prejudices. Man's basic sin, since the time of Adam, is that he has been trying to hide from God. Where better than in the church? But the Good News is that God will seek us out, even in church, and when He finds us, He deals with our prejudices.

The church can produce and has produced young men with totally opposing views of military service. One young man, by reading his Bible and asking for guidance, concludes that the message is clear, "Thou shalt not kill." He refuses to register for the draft, even though that means prison. Another young man reads in Paul's letter that our governors and officials are appointed by God and that we are to submit to their rule. He signs up for military service. Both of these young men may be God's sincere servants and yet they have very different ideas about what obedience means.

What then does it mean to be the church if there is no one set of requirements? In the second chapter of Acts, it seems to me we have a scriptural formula for what the church is meant to be. After the three thousand new converts joined the original one hundred and twenty (those who were in the Upper Room when the Spirit came), they "devoted themselves to the apostles' teaching and fellowship, to the breaking of bread and the prayers." I think those are still the essential ingredients of our life together.

First of all, the breaking of bread was and is a symbol of a historical event. You and I are stewards of that event. An event is something that happened, not a philosophy or a theology or an ethic. God was in Christ reconciling the world to Himself. God lived among us, was crucified by our hands, was raised, and now reigns as the Lord of the church. The breaking of bread celebrates that event. Jesus called the bread His body, broken for us. The wine is His blood, the blood of the new covenant. Every time we come to eucharist, or *agapē*, or holy communion, or mass, we celebrate an event. We bear witness to the event and we worship the event—not ideas about the event. And while the primary event is God in Christ—the incarnation, resurrection, and atonement— there are continuing events because as the apostles are doing in these verses, we pray to the God who is still among us. He is here. So there is the event that once happened and the events that continue to happen in your life and mine, as the God of the event continues to intervene.

Joseph Newton said some years ago, "When you become cynical about who God is, you then worship humanity. When you become cynical about humanity, you worship science. When you become cynical about science, you worship yourself." We have just come out of the great "me generation" of the seventies in which so many were practicing self-worship. Essential to our life together is the fact that we worship a God who was incarnate historically and who continues that incarnation in the lives of believers. You and I bear witness to both—event and events—whenever we pray and partake of the Lord's Supper.

The first Christians also devoted themselves to the apostles' doctrine. That initial, historical event and the events that continue happening need interpreting. The apostles' doctrine is necessary to explain what all this means. This is the purpose of theology, and we preach and teach concepts, rules, and doctrines about God and the faith.

But doctrine is lifeless without application, and that's where the apostolic fellowship comes in, which you and I are trying to re-cover. What does it mean? It is the life together that springs from the original event and the ongoing events and our convictions about them. Application includes both strategy for living and life style.

When I was on study leave in Greece, we visited Meteora, the scene of an amazing monastic movement of the twelfth through the seventeenth centuries. It was conceived at the same time that another monk, Saint Francis, was walking the Gospel into the poorest and most unlikely places in the world: slave camps, pirate ships, and leper colonies, among others. For Saint Francis, the application of the event meant bringing Christ on our two legs to the least and the last as well as the mighty. Meanwhile, the monks in Greece had a very different understanding of the application of the truth of the Gospel. They sought to withdraw from this evil world. They built monasteries on top of natural stone pillars one thousand feet high. They pulled themselves and their supplies up by means of ropes and baskets, and they lived there in total isola-tion. I'm sure they thought that was the best way to live in apostolic fellowship. We see here two totally different strategies, based on the same event and probably on similar interpretation.

This whole matter of strategy or application is still crucial for

Christians. We believe the gospel not only tells us why we live, but how to live. We have a concern for life style and we find in these verses a scriptural formula for authentic life style.

First of all, the life style is marked by power. God's people, then and now, have power to transmit to others discernible acts of grace, mercy, and healing. These are genuine signs and wonders, not ethereal and supernatural, but tangible medical, psychological, social results that amaze the nonbeliever. We read that fear came upon those who observed early Christians in all this. They weren't simply watching them going through nice, liturgical rites; they realized those early Christians had the power of God to transform and heal lives.

There are a growing number of people in our congregation in Seattle who have this kind of power. Sometimes, when the medical doctors or psychologists have been unable to help somebody in serious trouble, I get on the phone and ask two ladies to see that person. They have an effective ministry in "the healing of memories." They listen and pray, and often signs and wonders occur through these two faithful lay ministers. In the words of Scripture, "The kingdom of God does not consist in talk but in power" (1 Cor. 4:20). The power produces fear and awe, but it is one of the signs of authentic life together.

The apostolic life was also marked by joy. Acts 2:46 says they had "glad and generous hearts." They were praising the Lord—not because they had no problems, and not because there was no persecution. Not at all. Gladness and joy are the gifts of God, and those early Christians, who had at least as many problems as we do, were known for their joy and their gladness. In the Old Testament, God's faithful people came into His presence with gladness to sacrifice, to bring their gifts, to eat and drink before the Lord. I would not trust a dreary saint. Grimness is not a Christian virtue. And the dour, unblessed prophet who is pronouncing doom on the rest of us is more an Old Testament than a New Testament prophet.

Why is there not more joy in the world? It takes great courage to receive the gift of joy. It's easy to be miserable, depressed, unhappy, sorry for oneself—to engage in a kind of self-flagellation and go through life saying, "Nobody has it as bad as I do." We can justify all kinds of sins by reminding ourselves and others of how much we're suffering. God doesn't promise a rose garden, but He does promise the Holy Spirit. The gift of joy enables us to celebrate who we are, whose we are, the power that we have. And we celebrate that in the midst of incomplete, unfulfilled lives.

In his book *Anatomy of an Illness*, Norman Cousins tells about the power of joy as a therapeutic force. The medical world is now confirming his discovery. Doctors have said for years that you can't kill a happy man. They are saying, for the most part, that people are not unhappy because they are sick, but are sick because they are unhappy. Unhappiness is one of the initial causes of the breakdown of the body and spirit.

The apostles' fellowship was also marked by love. The genuine Christian life style is one of love, negotiable love, love that leads to generosity. The early Christians poured out their love in tangible ways. They brought all they had and gave it to the apostles, saying, "Here it is. Use it. We belong to a God of bountiful supply."

This attitude is the very opposite of the grasping tendency of the natural man. I am reminded of the two little boys who were fighting over a tricycle. Both were trying to ride it at the same time and finally one came up with a solution: "You know, if one of us would get off, I could have a lot more fun." While most of us abhor the attitude that what's yours is mine, we nevertheless feel justified in believing that what's mine is my own. But when God liberates us with His love, we begin to say to others, "What's mine is yours," because God's spirit within makes that attitude possible. We give because we belong to someone who first loved us. Generosity was a mark of the early church and it is a mark of the church today. Negotiable love to others in terms of substance, time, and caring is the mark of authenticity.

Apostolic fellowship resulted in community. Acts gives us a picture of the early church in which believers had all things in common. They lived together and broke bread together. They were persecuted together. They laughed together and they cried together and they shared all things as any had need. I don't think there is any institution in the world that compares with the church. We are unique. It is the only institution that I know of, anywhere, where we affirm we belong to one another and, at the same time, are encouraged to become more uniquely ourselves.

Most of life is designed to isolate us. We've invented all sorts of devices to encourage isolation, from peripatetic earphone radios to Pac-Man. All these gadgets encourage us to believe that we don't need anybody else. They are a way of saying, "I have my own world right here." When we are on occasion drawn out of our isolation into some cause or movement, the result can be a loss of personhood. We all wear the same uniform or label. We all sing the same songs. We think alike. We dress alike. We use the same deodorant and wear our hair the same way.

I'm always appalled by the accounts of the mass weddings the Moonies conduct, where thousands of couples are married simultaneously. They are all joined in one huge ceremony, every couple matched up by Mr. Moon himself. It looks like community, but it is a counterfeit, because any sense of personal identity is lost. Each bride and groom is part of some mass. Only in the church of Jesus Christ are we commanded to become the unique, unrepeatable miracle that God meant us to be at the same time that we draw closer together in fellowship. This unique community promises an end to isolation without the price of conformity. In this we find the seeds of God's healing for our fragmented society .

One of my favorite columnists, Ellen Goodman, who writes for the *Boston Globe*, calls us a "nation of leavers." Our forefathers left Asia or Europe to emigrate to America. Next, as the frontier opened, they moved west until they came to the other border. Now, with no place else to go, we are leaving each other. We have a need to move on from all the unfulfilled areas of our lives. The new frontier is God's community, a place where men and women and young people can begin to have intimacy and belong to one another. Only the church provides that kind of society, and it can become a source of new healing in the future decades of our country.

Chuck Colson says that the second most dramatic event of his life (the first was his introduction to Jesus Christ) occurred while he was serving time after the Watergate scandal. During that period, his family was having some serious problems, and the eighth-ranking member of the House of Representatives, a former political opponent and a member of Colson's prayer group, came up with an unusual proposal. The man asked the president's permission to serve out Colson's term. "His family needs him," he said. "Put me in his place." At that point Colson knew he belonged to a new kind of society. My wish for you is that you will belong to a handful of people in your church where that kind of unselfish generosity is possible. Like those first century Christians, we can say "What I have is yours. Let me give you what I have, whatever you need."

Dr. Joel Block, a psychological researcher, tells us that his studies indicate that only one man in five in America today has a real friend. Most of us have a few comrades that we work with, bowl with, go to football games with, or eat and drink with, but not a friend. Block claims only one man in five has someone to whom he can unburden his heart. If you're dying of loneliness, remember that the church is the only place which offers a loving community and where apostolic fellowship can be found.

Kenneth Chafin, a Southern Baptist minister and former professor of evangelism at Louisville Seminary, tells about one of the pivotal moments in his life. He grew up in a Christian home, part of a very poor farm family. One day one of their two workhorses died. His father continued his work stoically with the one remaining horse. Weeks later, Chafin found him behind the barn in tears of despair and bitterness, mourning his lost horse. "For the first time," he said, "I knew my father as a man to whom grief could come, a man who could be touched by a loss. Something happened between us when I saw my father weep." How much we need to see each other weep. We need to celebrate together, laugh, cry, pray. This is the beloved community, and these things can't happen in a crowd of thousands. They happen in groups of four, eight, or twelve, when we are on a pilgrimage together.

A member of our church, a sincere brother whom I love very much, said, "You know, I don't like these small groups you're getting us into." I said, "Who cares? You don't have to like them. If you are freezing to death, your best friend would make you get up and walk. It would be more comfortable to lie down and die, but a friend makes you do the painful thing that you might live. A lot of us are naturally shy. We don't want to get involved and share and care. But do it anyway—it's the route to life. The alternative is death." Until the church begins to produce little colonies like that, the church will not be the church. The church is the church when Jesus Christ, by the power of His Spirit, begins to produce the beloved community of people who are on an adventure.

I've had a letter in my file for a long time. It's written by a father to a favorite child. Here's what he says:

I sincerely wish you will have the experience of thinking up a new idea, planning it, organizing it, following it to completion, and having it be magnificently successful. I also hope you will go through the same process and have something bomb out. I wish you could know how it feels to run with all your heart and lose, horribly. I wish you could achieve some great good for mankind but have nobody know about it except you. I wish you could find something so worthwhile that you deem it worthy of the best of your life. I hope you become frustrated and challenged enough to begin to push back barriers of your personal limitations. I hope you make a stupid mistake and get caught redhanded and are big enough to say those magic words, "I was wrong." I wish for you a magnificent obsession that will give you reason for living and purpose and direction in life.

That's what one father wishes for his child. Our Heavenly Father wishes much more for us. And His church, the beloved family, is His means of helping us to find that magnificent obsession and live it out. Let the church be the church.

CHAPTER SIX

Basic Christianity

ACTS 3, 4

In trying to redefine the church and in searching for the basics, I have found that the Bible does not really give us a blueprint or manual in the sense of five rules or seven steps. That's probably just as well. I don't think we are supposed to put a dynamic, living relationship with God into a rigid mold.

The Wesleyan revival of the eighteenth century was one of the great outpourings of the Spirit, and the secret of that revival, aside from the holiness and dedication of the Wesleys and their followers, was the class meeting. All new converts attended class meetings where there was Bible reading and prayer. Healings took place and members were accountable to each other for their day-to-day Christian lives. After many years, John Wesley decided to write a guide for these class meetings, and a manual for class leadership was published. The power and vitality of the movement seemed to diminish from that point on. It seems there is no learned technique for being the people of God. The only source we have is the Spirit Himself.

It is therefore with some trepidation that I would suggest that in chapters 3 and 4 of the Book of Acts, we find some biblical principles on basic Christianity—authentic ingredients of the true church. First of all, there is the *giving of self*. In the opening incident in chapter 3, we read that Peter and John, going in to worship, met a beggar at the gate of the temple, a beggar who had been there for many years. He had been lame from birth and was asking for alms. The Jews believed then, as we do now, that there is blessing in helping the unfortunate. The beggar was in the habit of receiving alms and gifts. Peter and John had something else in mind. They said, "Wait a minute. Silver and gold have we none, but such as we have we give you. In the name of Jesus, stand up and walk." The beggar leapt up and praised God and the people were amazed.

The implication seems clear that money cannot substitute for personal involvement if we are to take seriously the needs of those around us. We have built all sorts of institutions with our tax money and our Christian tithes and offerings to feed and house and care for the sick, the poor, and the unfortunate. Once that's done, we tend to feel our obligations end. "Don't trouble us. There are places for people like you."

Just recently in downtown Seattle I was hurrying to a meeting when I noticed someone coming toward me, ready to make a "touch." He was a fairly young man, but with the look and smell of a panhandler. I found myself saying, "I hope he doesn't stop *me*. I'm late." That's not what Peter and John did. They said, "We don't have silver and gold to deal with your problem. All we have is ourselves and our faith." Peter and John took the beggar and his problems seriously—quite the reverse of what I found myself wanting to do. They stopped and took time with this man. They honored him and loved him. They must have prayed with him and for him, and he was healed. This giving of self is essential to basic Christianity.

I'm always interested in the tests that psychologists and psychiatrists rig up to try to determine which school of counseling is most effective—nondirective, Freudian, gestalt, transactional analysis, or a score of other approaches. These different techniques are used on groups with similar problems, juvenile delinquents, drug addicts, the emotionally disturbed, and the depressed. As part of the experiment there is always a control group, made up of counselors who are not professionals—airline pilots, homemakers, secretaries or salesmen. Invariably, the control group gets the same results as the professionals. We can guess why. Power for healing is released when you and I simply focus on somebody else unhurriedly, taking him or her seriously and listening. The problem is that we are all so focused on our own concerns we don't take time to do this.

Dr. Seymour Diamond recently did some research on family problems and he came up with conclusions that are devastating for those of us who are fathers. He claims that today's average American father gives undivided attention to his children thirty-eight seconds a day. He gives them partial attention for twenty minutes while he is otherwise engaged, watching TV or working on some project. Diamond is saying that if we are to love our children, there must be significant times in the day when they are listened to and focused on. In short, we fathers (and mothers!) must give ourselves.

Sometimes we hesitate to give of ourselves because we feel so personally bankrupt—emotionally, spiritually, and otherwise. When Moses was chosen by God to lead the Israelites out of Egypt, he felt he was not prepared or equipped. God said to Moses, "What is in your hand?" "Only a shepherd's staff," Moses replied, and God said that was enough. God would ask us the same question, "What is in your hand right now?" Whatever you have in your hand, youth or old age, sickness or health, pain or pleasure, wealth or poverty, God will use it if you are willing to give yourself to others.

Last year one woman in our congregation lost her huband, a wonderful Christian man. She has since gathered together a group of other recent widows to support and pray for each other. Miracles are happening as they are giving themselves to each other. As

Christians, we are to invest ourselves in others and that's even better than investing our money. We can't warehouse all the afflicted and needy. As God's family, we must say as Peter and John did, "Such as I have I give you."

Essential to basic Christianity is *the preaching of Jesus*. When the begger was healed, the people were amazed and many were converted by witnessing this extraordinary event. Peter did not let it go at that. He preached the second Christian sermon. He was saying, in essence, "Wait a minute. Don't thank us. We're not doctors or rabbis. Jesus did this. We simply called on His name." Peter preached Jesus, and that is still our message, not just from the pulpit on Sunday but through our lives and witness on Monday, Tuesday, and Wednesday.

The next mark of authentic Christianity is *opposition*. The text here tells us Christians can expect opposition. Everybody will not cheer because you are giving yourself and proclaiming Jesus. There will be opposition. In Luke 6:26 we read, "Woe to you, when all men speak well of you, for so their fathers did to the false prophets." If you are by nature a people-pleaser, like me, you want everybody to think you're wonderful. I need to be reminded often that if everybody thinks I'm wonderful I'm in serious trouble in terms of being an effective witness. If I'm really about my Father's business, there'll be opposition.

Boldness is another mark of the early church. The disciples courted risk and danger. They went into situations they knew would be dangerous. When they were released from prison they went right back into those dangerous situations. When they defended themselves before the religious authorities, they confounded their hearers, who were amazed by these common, uneducated men. Uneducated doesn't mean illiterate. Uneducated means they were not rabbis but laymen. Professional preachers and teachers who had been to seminary were being confounded by ordinary laymen and they didn't like it. A lot of us preachers today don't like it, but that's our problem. The hope of the church is still a bold, witnessing laity.

Witness is still an ingredient of basic Christianity. The disciples witnessed, not to a theology or doctrine or the Scriptures, but to an event. The event was that God was in Christ reconciling the world to Himself. Jesus came and lived among us. He was crucified and raised from the dead and He lives in us by the power of the Spirit. The disciples could say, like the blind man whom Jesus healed, "One thing I know. Whereas I was blind, now I see." They bore witness wherever they went to the Lord Jesus.

Corporate worship is another essential of basic Christianity. It has been for almost two thousand years now. We come from busy lives or broken lives, full lives or empty ones, from joy or sadness. We come from ministering in the highways and byways to pray and thank God in the company of His people. When we come together for worship, we are healed and transformed, inadvertently, because God is there.

Finally, the early church was a true *community*. Community is still a mark of authentic Christianity. The last verses of chapter 4 in the Book of Acts tell us that those early believers had all things in common. Their possessions were not their own. When we can say, "What's mine is yours," we really are a family. I know I said earlier that money won't do it, that we must give ourselves. Nevertheless, unless we are willing to give our money to the common good to be used in ministry and mission, we will not have community. Unselfish giving is a requirement.

I love the statement Pope Pius IV made on learning of the death of John Calvin. He said, "The power of that heretic lay in the fact that he was indifferent to money." I would wish that same kind of heresy for all of us. When we begin to say, "I have a heavenly Father who will supply my needs; I am His partner in life; I can take from my storehouse and bring it into His," then community results.

Richard Leakey, famous archeologist who worked in northern Kenya, commented in his book *People of the Lake* about what separated man from the apes. He said it was not our intelligence, but our generosity. Our ability to share sets us apart. We are made in God's image, unlike the animals, and we have a capacity for generosity. Jesus Christ came to make us truly human, and He meant for us to be whole persons—generous persons. In community, we share with each other and with the world.

But the real key to the power of the church is in the last verses of chapter 4, where we read about Barnabas. His real name was Joseph but he was nicknamed Barnabas, which meant "Son of Encouragement." He was the person who invariably came up with words of encouragement: "You can do it. You're going to make it. Don't give up now. I'm betting on you." I hope you have had one or more Barnabases in your life—a teacher, scoutmaster, friend, relative, someone who came alongside and believed in you. Hoover Rupert tells of a time in his life when he was down and out and uncertain he could go on, when an old preacher came along and said, "Son, just remember that God has a bigger stake in your life than you will ever know." That was a turning point for Rupert. God has an enormous stake in your life as well. How much we need the Barnabas person to remind us of that.

Abraham Vereide, founder of International Christian Leadership and the Presidential Prayer Breakfasts, was one of those Barnabas people. I can remember being with him in Bermuda on one occasion when he wandered into the government building where the parliament met. He popped into that roomful of officials— men and women he had never seen before—and said something like this, "God bless you. You're doing a great job. Keep it up. I'm proud of you." He walked out, leaving them all slightly dazed. That was Abraham Vereide's style in all sorts of situations. As for me, I'd like to make Barnabas the patron saint of our congregation in Seattle. How much we need such people around us, believing in us and encouraging us.

Pearl Mesta, Washington's most famous hostess, was once asked about the secret of her success. She said, "It's easy. It's all done in the way you greet people as they come and as they go. As they come, I say to each one, 'Oh, at last you're here.' And as they go, I say, 'Do you really have to leave so soon?'" Why don't you try that at your next party and see what happens? It could even work at church! This is the Barnabas syndrome. Barnabas brought that dimension to the early church.

I heard a pertinent story about Darrell Royal, football coach at the University of Texas for many years and now athletic director. At the beginning of his coaching career there, he got a call from an alumnus after his first game. The man was a generous contributor and part of the booster club. "Darrell," he said, "I want to know when I can see you and give you some constructive criticism." "Never!" was the reply. "What do you mean?" asked the alumnus. "We have a group of men here who get together after every game and figure out what went wrong. For years we have been giving the coach constructive criticism. Don't you want constructive criticism?" "No, I don't work well that way," said Royal. "I work best by friendship, by affirmation, by support and appreciation. Tell me when I'm doing something right and cheer for me. Please don't tell me when I'm failing. I already know that." Apparently the alumni group learned how to cheer, and as they did Texas became one of the all-time great teams.

I was with Maggie Kuhn, head of the Grey Panthers, at a meeting recently, and she told us some interesting facts about sandhill cranes. It seems these large birds, who commute great distances and traverse continents, have three remarkable qualities. First of all, they rotate leadership. No one bird stays out in front all the time. Second, they choose a leader who can handle turbulence. And then, all during the time one bird is leading, the rest are honking, signaling their affirmation. That's not a bad model for the church. Certainly we need leaders who welcome turbulence and who are aware that leadership ought to be rotated. But most of all, we need a church where we are all honking encouragement. That's the Barnabas syndrome.

CHAPTER SEVEN

Problems in Paradise

ACTS 5, 6

The fourth chapter of Acts ends with a description of the
ideal church, one in which everybody shares what he or
she has. There is power and healing. The believers are of one
mind and one heart, and they rejoice and celebrate. This ideal
church sounds very much like Paradise. But in the very next
chapter, we find that in that perfect church there were some imperfect people.

Sometimes I wonder why Luke had to include the events of the
fifth chapter. Why not go on to the sixth chapter and leave us with
chapter 4's ideal picture of the church? This sort of incongruous
juxtaposition is, to me, the authenticating mark of the Bible.
Unlike any other religious book, it does not idealize life. All was
not rosy and wonderful. The Bible, the book of ultimate reality,
describes who we are. It tells it like it is: God's people are frail and
feeble and sometimes downright dishonest.

Chapter 5 presents us with three problems in this paradise of the early church. First of all, we find that two card-carrying, dues-paying, born-again, Spirit-filled Christians drop dead in church. That's the kind of problem that could really discourage membership. The second problem is that non-card-carrying, non-dues-paying, non-Christians are hanging around the church in great numbers getting healed. Next, we find there is jealousy in the household of faith. There is jealousy as God seems to be using one person and not another. It's understandable. It's still hard to say "Amen" at somebody else's prayer meeting.

It seems to me we can learn from this clinical description of the early church and its problems and apply what we learn to our own church situations today. Let's begin with problem number one—Ananias and Sapphira. Money is the cause of the problem. Money is strange stuff. In itself it is amoral, neither good nor bad. The rich are not necessarily wicked and the poor not necessarily good. But money is often a barometer of our lives and values. My attitude toward money tells you a great deal about me. If you looked at my checkbook and learned how I spent my money, you'd have some solid clues about the extent of my spirituality.

Years ago, Joe Louis, former world heavyweight boxing champion, said, "I don't like money, actually, but it quiets my nerves." We can all relate to that. In hard times, a bank account or some prudent investments certainly produce quieter nerves. Some time ago I read something that Picasso said about money that puzzled me and still does. He said, "I would like to be a rich man who lives like a poor man." As for me, I would rather be a poor man who lives like a rich man. That makes real sense. I'd like to live well without the bother of having to manage and care about money, but as I said, our attitude about money is revealing.

Ananias and Sapphira join this first Christian church in which everybody is filled with grace and the believers have all things in common, their security resting no longer in money, but in God. Barnabas and the others sell all they have and share it with the whole community. Ananias and Sapphira, wanting to be a part of all this, sell a field and pretend to give all the proceeds, when in fact, they keep back half. When their deceit is discovered, Ananias drops dead and Sapphira follows him forthwith.

One of our adult education classes was studying the Book of Acts recently and this chapter was being discussed. The question came up, as it always does, "Why did God kill Ananias and Sapphira?" One young lawyer in the class said, "There is no way to defend God's actions here. The punishment far outweighs the crime." I believe the real question is, did God kill Ananias and Sapphira? And I think the answer is both yes and no. For example, let's say you try to prove to a friend that there is a God by stepping off the balcony on the twentieth floor of some building. You will certainly crash to your death, but did God kill you? Yes and no. God invented the law of gravity and it certainly did a job on you. In one sense, God's law killed you. But did God kill you vindictively for your effrontery? Certainly not.

I'd like to make a case for God in this whole matter of Ananias and Sapphira. At least three significant factors are involved in their untimely death. First of all, they were under extreme stress. Doctors tell us that the number one killer today is stress, and one serious cause of stress is our attempt to pretend to be something we're not, to try to misrepresent ourselves. Perhaps we've been promoted in our job and find we're way over our head. If the truth were known, I suspect most of us are way over our heads. That doesn't have to be a problem unless we must pretend we are adequate, and we try to look cool and fake it. The stress level increases when we have to pretend to be competent or pretend to be good or pretend to be generous, which is what happened with Ananias and Sapphira. They said, "We're as committed as the rest of you. All we have is the Lord's." It's possible the stress brought about by their own pretense or hypocrisy killed them.

The word *hypocrisy* comes from the Greek word meaning "to wear a mask." In Greek drama, the actors put on masks to convey emotions—happy masks and sad masks. A hypocrite is someone whose goodness or generosity or kindness is a mask. If we live this way long enough, the stress builds up and the body begins to suffer.

I heard recently about a clergyman who had a call from the IRS. They wanted to know if it was true that a certain member of the congregation had contributed thirty-five hundred dollars to the church that year. "I'd rather not respond to that question right now," said the clergyman. "But if you will call me back tomorrow, I'm sure I can reply affirmatively." When we begin to practice deception, whether or not the law or the IRS ever finds us out, our own hearts condemn us. It's a way of living that one of my young friends would call xylocephalic—that is, wooden-headed. Xylocephalic living is pretending to be something that you're not.

In contrast to the Ananias and Sapphira story, the Bible indicates that God is extraordinarily easy on sinners. He assumes that we will sin. We are not to do so willingly or blatantly, but if we obey the Great Commandment to love God with our whole heart and our neighbor as ourself, we will occasionally sin by omission and commission. The pressure or stress comes when we pretend we're not sinners, that we're beyond that level and are sinners emeritus. But in the first chapter of the first letter of John, we are instructed to walk in the light. We are to be who we are, open before our brothers and sisters in the faith. We are to do our good works in secret and confess our sins publicly.

Charles Lamb once said, "The greatest pleasure I know is to do a good action by stealth and have it found out by accident." We all love that feeling—to have some act of charity that only God knows about come to light. We say, "Shucks, it wasn't anything," but we are secretly pleased.

I think a second factor in the death of Ananias and Sapphira was their sense of being cut off. The two key words today in medical science are stress and loneliness. Loneliness has nothing to do with being alone. You can be alone and have a full life. I know some recent widows and widowers who are discovering all kinds of resources for living because of enforced aloneness. Loneliness comes when you feel cut off from other people. Perhaps the person you love has abandoned you, or you have abandoned him or her. You suffer isolation or cut-offness when you have broken a covenant and betrayed a friend, a business partner, or spouse.

For Ananias and Sapphira, this first-century church was perhaps the single most important thing in their lives. The church members were their family. Jesus said, "Whoever does the will of my Father in heaven is my brother, and sister, and mother" (Matt. 12:50). This frail family of the church is the most mysterious and powerful creation in the world. It is Jesus' own family. Ananias and Sapphira came before the most significant group in their lives with lies and deceit. They broke the covenant and their grief was enormous. Just the fear of being found out could certainly have killed them. There is a true story about a courtier of Edward I who on one occasion incurred the king's wrath. The unfortunate man died on the spot, just like Ananias and Sapphira. He loved the king and had failed him. The king's good will was so essential to him that he dropped dead when it was withheld.

Can you remember a time like that in your own life, of being found out or caught off base by somebody you loved? I can remember my first time very vividly. I was seven years old and I had been smoking cigarettes out in the alley. I came into our Chicago apartment to find my mother having coffee with four or five ladies. Swedes tend to do that all day long. I said, "Hi." She said, "What's in your pocket?" I said, "Nothing!" She said, "Show me what's in your pocket," and I pulled out my package of cigarettes. I thought I would die right there in our living room. I was sure I had betrayed my mother irrevocably. If you increase this emotion manyfold you have some appreciation for what happened to Ananias and Sapphira.

The third significant factor here is Peter's judgment. We find that Peter lowered the boom on these cheaters with no equivocation. Now, you put together stress and cut-offness and a judgmental preacher who is dispensing anything but grace, and that's a pretty heavy combination. No wonder Ananias and Sapphira died. Peter's attitude in the situation was so unlike Jesus' own attitude. When Jesus came upon the adulteress about to be stoned, he shamed her accusers into leaving and said, "Neither do I condemn you, but go and sin no more." To the thief on the cross, Jesus promised eternal life. That's grace. All of us who are xylocephalics are forgiven, but we are to repent and change.

I meet with a group of men each week to read the Bible and pray. As we came to this portion of Acts a few weeks ago, one of the

men said, "I think Peter's attitude was all wrong." In an earlier
chapter I suggested that one title for the Book of Acts might be
"The Mistakes of Peter and Paul," and I don't believe we are to
consider this account as giving us a model way to treat all hypo-
crites and deceivers. I believe Peter learned from this incident, and
later on we see him behaving with more charity. Nevertheless, in
this case, the combination of stress and loneliness and judgment
resulted in two people dropping dead.

A second problem for the early church, as I pointed out earlier,
concerned the nonbelievers who came around and were healed.
There was no healing service *à la* Oral Roberts. There was no
laying on of hands and no anointing with oil. The sick simply
hung around Christians who were living in the power of the Spirit,
celebrating and worshiping, and they all got well. We would call
that pre-evangelism. God got their attention. Something discernible began to happen to them.

Again, we're told that the number one factor in illness is life
style. If we have satisfying work and loving relationships and if our
life has purpose and meaning, our body responds. Now what did
those who came to this first Christian church find? They found a
fellowship of people who loved unconditionally. They found hope
and caring and generosity. They found acceptance. They found
joy. They could for the first time publicly confess their sins. All the
things that make for health were by-products of the life style of the
first Christians. There is no more therapeutic force in the world
than to be around those whose lives manifest the fruits of the
Spirit. Before they knew about Jesus, God changed their lives and
they were healed.

The third problem, as I said, was jealousy. The Christians then
were still considered Jews. The faith had not yet spread to the
Gentiles. The Sadducees, the rulers and high priests, were disap-
proving. Multitudes were finding God and health but the authorities were skeptical. They were saying, "If this renewal and
revival is not happening through us, it's not acceptable." How
unlike the Apostle Paul's attitude! He tells us in Philippians
1:15–18 that although people are preaching Jesus from all kinds of

mixed motives, he doesn't care, as long as Jesus is preached. He is not jealous. He rejoices!

We still have to learn to deal with jealousy in the household of faith. When Billy Graham comes to town, not every Christian church supports him, although he packs every local arena and gives his hearers a chance to accept Jesus. How can anyone be against that? But as we all know, there is invariably some degree of opposition. As we said, if it's not my prayer meeting, I have a hard time saying "Amen"!

In the midst of this opposition, Gamaliel, one of the Pharisees, was a voice of reason. He suggested to the council that they wait and see what happened before they made a judgment. He suggested a pragmatic test. "Are these new Christians producing shalom, or wholeness? If so, God is in it. If God is not in it, this new movement will die of natural causes. Let's not be found opposing God Himself." That was Gamaliel's advice.

How much we need this kind of openness in the church. I heard this week about a Russian and American who were discussing their two countries. The American said, "Well, after all, we have free speech and you don't. I could stand up in the middle of Washington, D.C., and say, 'The President of the United States is a jerk.'" The Russian said, "Why, we have that same kind of free speech. I can stand in the middle of Red Square and say, 'The President of the United States is a jerk.'" Those of us in the church need to have a permissive spirit. We need to withhold judgment on those ministering in Jesus' name and wait to examine their fruits.

Ananias and Sapphira wanted to have it all. They wanted to live in two worlds and have the best of both. They sought riches or security first, and that was their downfall. The challenge for Christians is to seek first the Kingdom of God. If we seek it second, we had best get out of the Kingdom business. Seeking God's Kingdom is not something we add to an already-busy schedule. Jesus warns us to seek *first* the Kingdom of God, and everything we need will be ours (Matt. 6:33).

CHAPTER EIGHT

The Price of Glory

ACTS 7

Perhaps at some point in your life you have considered
writing your autobiography. You may not produce a
best-seller, but nevertheless, you could come up with an important history to pass on to your progeny. One way to outline such a
biography would be to devote a chapter each to all the times in
your life when you were chosen. The idea of being chosen is
central to the biblical message. God chose us. Before we loved
Him, He first loved us. After creating all the galaxies, He chose to
visit one little insignificant planet in a tiny solar system called
Earth. He chose to enter into human life in the person of His Son.
Before that incarnational visit, He chose a people through whom
to reveal Himself to the rest of the world, the Jews. He chose Mary
through whom the Messiah came. In time He chose you and me,
the new Israel, to be His instruments of revelation and reconcilia-
tion.

Being chosen is something all of us covet. It is one of life's greatest experiences. We dream that the right person will choose us as a marriage partner or as a friend. We hope to be chosen for a particular job or for some specific group or assignment. Somehow all of life's dreams are tied up with being chosen, and that means we have to deal with our pain and disappointment when we are *not* chosen, or when being chosen results in suffering or disillusionment.

Lately I've been outlining my own autobiography in terms of those chosen moments. My first memory of being chosen came in third grade when I was made a blackboard monitor, not because I was a model student, but because my parents wined and dined my teacher. When I got the privilege of cleaning the blackboards, I thought I had arrived . . . until my classmates began to call me "teacher's pet." My new status was a mixed blessing. My next triumph came in sixth grade when I was chosen to be a member of the safety patrol. I could wear that white belt and a badge and order my fellow fifth and sixth graders to stop and start at will at street crossings. However, I also bore, with the other patrol members, the stigma of the establishment. At recess we were often teased and avoided. Being chosen, again, had its bitter side.

Later, as a member of my high school football team, I dreamed of someday being chosen for the starting lineup. The day finally came when the coach read off the names of the starting team and said, "Larson, right tackle." This was my glorious moment, except I was well aware that the first and second string right tackles were both out with injuries. Furthermore, we were soundly defeated. Then there was the junior prom. Of all the girls I knew, I wanted most of all to go with Marjorie. Marjorie said, "Yes," and this was a triumph. She had chosen me to be her date—except I learned later that she really wanted to go with my friend, who had asked somebody else. She was going with me in order to be near my friend. I felt like that young man who said to his girlfriend, "Darling, I don't have a sailboat and a sports car like Jerome, but I love you with all my heart." "I love you too, dear," she replied, "but tell me more about Jerome."

As you think of the chosen moments in your life, there is sometimes pain involved. Perhaps you were chosen for a job to which you aspired and then found yourself in over your head and fearful that someone would discover how inadequate you were. Often even when we reach our chosen goals, we live with this dread of failure. Even in marriage we find ourselves caught in this dichotomy. Having chosen the one person in all the world we want to live with, we find ourselves repeatedly failing that person, not being what he or she seems to want or need.

Even more painful are the times when we were not chosen. What is God saying to us in those times? My most vivid memory of such a time concerned a girl I met in high school, a marvelous Christian girl, who believed in me and who was a great influence in my life for the two years we dated. I went off to World War II deeply in love with Jean. I served in the infantry in France and Germany, and I still remember the day when, after two weeks of fierce fighting in freezing weather, the trailers pulled in with hot meals and blankets and mail from home. I had a letter from Jean saying, "Dear Bruce: I hate to have to write this, but I have met a wonderful man here in college and we're going to be married." There I sat up to my belly button in water in a miserable foxhole without a drain plug, thinking, "How could you do this to me, Lord?" Little did I know that God had someone else in mind for me, even then. It's hard to believe that when your heart is breaking.

I was converted during the war and came home wanting to be a preacher. I had my heart set on going to the University of Chicago, but I was too late. They were filled. I went instead to a small Presbyterian school in Lake Forest, Illinois, where I met many friends who have shaped my life, including my old friend Lloyd Ogilvie, pastor of the Hollywood Presbyterian Church.

Recently I had a speaking date in Chicago and my wife and I decided to fulfill a lifelong dream to travel across our great country by train. We boarded the Empire Builder in Seattle Thursday night, had dinner, and went to sleep to that wonderful clickety-clack sound of the rails. We got up Friday morning and headed for the dining car, which, incidentally, was a far cry from the dining cars of my youth. Their impeccable service, gleaming silver, and white tablecloths have now been replaced by radar range food on plastic trays and a paper plate. Nevertheless, we were enjoying the whole experience.

As we sat over coffee, the train pulled into a station at the east end of Glacier National Park and the trainman called the name of the town. To my amazement, it was the town in which I was supposed to have taken my first parish some thirty years ago, shortly after my graduation from seminary. Hazel and I were married in my senior year at seminary, and during that year a pulpit committee came to Princeton and hired me to pastor their small church in Montana. We were to start in June, but in the meantime, we found ourselves expecting a child that summer and so I asked if we could delay our arrival somewhat. The committee said, "No, thanks. Out here it starts snowing by August 15, and the season is over. If you can't come early in the summer, don't come at all." And so I was rejected—unchosen. I went instead to Binghamton, New York.

Now here we were all those years later, looking out of a train window at that very town, the most dismal, forlorn, bleak-looking place I think I have ever seen. We said almost simultaneously, "Oh, Lord, thank you." Until that moment we had been unaware of what we had been spared. We had been given an unusual opportunity to see the road not taken, and I couldn't help thinking that when we die we will all have the opportunity of looking back at the wake of our lives with new appreciation. We will understand anew the grace of God, not only in those times of being chosen, but in all those times when we didn't get the job we wanted, we didn't marry the person we wanted, we did not receive the honor or place we coveted. That chance stop on the Empire Builder gave Hazel and me an awareness of all the things God had saved us from.

The biblical record indicates that the price of being chosen is usually suffering. The Jews are chosen people who have suffered as perhaps no other single group. In the Broadway musical *Fiddler on the Roof*, the hero, Tevye, says at one point, "O Lord, couldn't you choose somebody else for a while? I'm tired of being your chosen person." Mary is chosen and pays a great price. When she brings her baby to the temple for the rite of purification she meets the old prophet, Simeon. Holding the baby, he tells her that he has now seen the salvation of Israel, but he also says that a sword will pierce her heart. Both were accurate prophecies.

In the seventh chapter of Acts, we find Stephen being chosen as the first deacon. He was chosen to correct problems in the young church. Food and benefits were not being distributed equitably, and discord and jealousy had resulted. Stephen had excellent credentials, being full of wisdom and the Holy Spirit and of good reputation. He was so good and so powerful that he was an offense, and before long he was brought to trial and martyred. He suffered a premature death by stoning. (There is no guarantee you'll live a long life if you're chosen.) In death, Stephen saw the glory of God. We read that Saint Paul was there, in the person of Saul, watching and consenting to this unjust execution, and surely Saul was never the same again.

Being chosen means both glory and suffering. Scott Peck, a psychiatrist, has written a book entitled *The Road Less Traveled*. Interestingly enough, he became a Christian after writing the book. The very first sentences are intriguing. "Life is difficult," he says. "Once you accept that fact, then it is no longer difficult." We tend to think that being chosen by God means we'll be spared any suffering. In John 8:36 Jesus says, "If the Son makes you free, you will be free indeed." Free from suffering? Not at all. But we no longer have *purposeless* suffering. We can be like Stephen, who suffered unjustly because he was chosen, but saw beyond those sufferings to God's great purposes in the world. We too can bring glory to suffering and make it work for us.

Yet we are not to seek suffering. For hundreds of years there has been a strange heresy in the Christian church which implies that suffering is noble, and that the more you suffer, the more you are like Jesus. To glorify suffering is heresy. Nevertheless, suffering may come, often undeservedly, as it did for Stephen. Don't waste your suffering; turn it into glory. In the middle of his persecution,

Stephen, "full of the Holy Spirit, gazed into heaven and saw the glory of God, and Jesus standing at the right hand of God" (Acts 7:55). That vision did not change the suffering. Rather, it transformed the sufferer.

There are Stephens in the church in every century. Recently, the Roman Catholic Church canonized a new saint very deservedly. Maximilian Kolbe, a Franciscan priest imprisoned at Auschwitz, was one of the many who suffered in the holocaust under the Nazi regime. When, in July 1941, one of the prisoners escaped, the commandant called all six hundred inmates out of their barracks. He announced that ten prisoners would die in retribution, and he walked down the line arbitrarily selecting those ten. "You and you and you." When the ten had been chosen Father Kolbe stepped forward with a request. "Sir, may I take the place of one of these ten?" The commandant agreed. Father Kolbe replaced one man in the line of ten. They were sentenced to starve to death in a stone dungeon.

The records of their last days indicate that there was no complaining. There was joy! They sang hymns of praise to God. One by one they succumbed to starvation until only four were left. There was such a mysterious, powerful aura around that dungeon that the guards refused even to go near it. Father Kolbe was the last to die, almost as though he had been commissioned to help the other nine die with grace. When, after three weeks, he still lived, he was killed with an injection of carbolic acid. Father Kolbe found the same glory in suffering as Stephen, the first martyr.

You and I have a unique opportunity when life crashes in on us. We have a chance to say, "Lord, let me use this circumstance." We can become wounded healers, to use Henri Nouwen's phrase—those who have borne great sorrow with such grace that we are God's resource for others.

CHAPTER NINE

Illogical Priorities

ACTS 8

It would seem that there are at least three distinctive characteristics of the infant church described for us in the Book of Acts, and those characteristics are still marks of the true church. First of all, the men and women who make up the church, its living stones, are very frail and fallible. That was true in the first century, and still is. That's part of the whole mystery of the church. Second, the genius of the church, the power and the wisdom of the church, rests in the Holy Spirit who is among us. We are His creation. We are on His timetable. We are empowered by Him. The early church experienced the wind and fire of God, the power and presence of God, and we are still experiencing that same Spirit. Third, the true church, then and now, proclaims the Kingdom of God. The Kingdom has come, and you and I have the power to invite others into that Kingdom and to say, "Come in if you will. You are welcome. God cares about you."

In the eighth chapter of Acts, we find three separate scenes of a continuing drama. Each is a demonstration of what I would call the illogical priorities of the church, and all seem to point up the frailty and fallibility of God's people as well as the overriding power of the Holy Spirit.

Scene one is set in Jerusalem. This early band of Christians had one simple creed: "Jesus is Lord." They had been commissioned by this same Lord on more than one occasion to "go . . . into all the world and preach the gospel to every nation." Yet in this post-Pentecost period, they simply sat in Jerusalem, enjoying sweet fellowship. Their priorities don't seem very logical. They believed Jesus to be Lord, head of the church, King of the universe, and yet they ignored His orders to "go." We are still disobedient people, all caught up in our own concerns, and yet God can move us in His own way and in His own time.

The early Christians were egotists, just as we are. An egotist is some clod who is more interested in himself than he is in you or me. We are egotists who are more interested in our agenda than in God's. "What about *me?* What do *I* get out of all this? Let me tell you *my* story." God may have to wait to get our attention, but He will get it. We're like the lady who went to the doctor and asked, "What can I do to feel better without giving up what's making me feel so bad?" Even in the Kingdom we are guilty of mixed motives. Caught up in our own agendas, we say, "Here I am, send me—but, of course, before you do, I have my job, my committees, my social life." We are self-centered, self-seeking people, but God is big enough to deal with that problem. He can use circumstances to force us into being His people and doing His will. In spite of the illogical priorities of the early Christians, when the persecution arose which scattered them, they inadvertently brought the gospel to Samaria and Judea.

Scene two finds them in Samaria, where they had fled for their very lives. It's interesting to note that in those pre-Freudian days, they spent no time wallowing in guilt. They were supposed to have moved out on their own steam, but instead they did so for selfish motives, trying to save their lives. Instead of taking their pulse and

saying, "We failed again. We are unprofitable servants," they
plunged into ministry. Philip, the evangelist, began to proclaim
the Good News to the people of Samaria.

We have much to learn from their attitude. If we can get beyond
worrying about our motives, God can still work through us. It
doesn't really matter how we got to the place we're in now. It
doesn't even matter what our motive was in becoming a Christian.
It may have been to please a sweetheart, our spouse, or our parents. It doesn't matter whether or not we had a high motive for
joining the part of the church we're in now. God has us there and
He can use us. Whatever mixed motives got us into the Kingdom
and into ministry, we're here now. We can use the place we are in
to proclaim the Good News.

That's what Philip did. He just began to proclaim the Good
News, and as he did, his hearers were delivered from all kinds of
unclean spirits. It's still happening. Week by week I have the
privilege of meeting those who have been delivered from alcoholism, from irresponsible sexuality, from crippling inhibitions of all
kinds, from mental or emotional problems. I recently met a group
of people delivered from cults. For the first time, they had heard
the Good News about Jesus and become liberated. Verse 8 of
chapter 8 tells us, "There was much joy in that city." Philip
brought them Good News.

We need not be embarrassed to bring Good News. Recently I
conducted a wedding during which the groom asked me to preach
a sermon for all the friends and guests. He even gave me a four-
point outline. That was a first for me, and I wasn't sure I was up to
it. But the point is that this young couple wanted those near and
dear to them to hear the Good News. They wanted their wedding
guests to learn something about the goodness of the God who was
uniting them in marriage.

We need not feel embarrassed about sharing good news. If
evangelism is hard for you, perhaps the message you're sharing is
not good news. God's nature is like two sides of the same coin, with
judgment on one side and grace on the other. We can emphasize
His judgment. We can say, "Shape up. If you don't get with it and

meet the Lord, you're done for." That's perfectly true, but it's not good news. On the other side of the same coin is God's love. You can tell a troubled friend, "Whatever mess you're in right now, if you're depressed, in trouble, if you've lost your health, your spouse or your job, God is on your side. He loves you."

A few years ago, while we were living in Florida, a friend called and said, "Bruce, I've been reading your books and I understand you believe in spiritual healing." I said, "I sure do. I've seen God's miracles." Then he mentioned the very sick young daughter of some mutual friends in town. "I have been told she's dying," he said, "and I just called the family to ask if you and Hazel and my wife and I could come over tomorrow and pray for her healing." I was less than eager. The whole scheme seemed a little pushy. "Don't you believe in healing?" he asked. I told him we'd be there.

The next day we went. Now this man is a manufacturer of heavy machinery and not exactly a "spiritual type," but he is a man full of the Holy Spirit. My friend announced our intentions right off to the young woman. "We came to pray for you. We believe Jesus wants to make you well." As we prayed, I confess I mostly felt uncomfortable and somewhat of an intruder. But within a month the young woman began to improve. The point is that even when we get into those places we wouldn't have chosen, we can expect God to use us there. Instead of asking, "What am I doing here?" we can say, "Lord, there's a need here. I'm going to proclaim Good News."

Philip performed signs and wonders, and Simon the magician, seeing all this, wanted that same power. Unfortunately, he tried to buy the power of the Holy Spirit, which is a gift of God, a free gift. It is understandable that Simon wanted that gift for himself, for it would have made him rich to be able to bring this same remarkable healing to others. I'm sure most of those in medical and psychiatric fields would love to have the gift of spiritual healing. It would make them a fortune. But that gift is not for sale. When Simon aspired to the gift, Peter said, almost literally, "You and your money may go to hell." But, unlike Ananias and Sapphira, Simon was given a second chance, a chance to repent and to change. Peter apparently had begun to deal with sinners with more charity. And we would like to believe that Simon becomes a believer full of the Holy Spirit, giving away freely the gift he had freely received.

Peter and John finally came up from Jerusalem because they heard that a revival was going on, a revival among these "half-breed" Samaritans. The Samaritans had intermarried with Gentiles and therefore were not pure Jews, genetically. The Jews were contemptuous of them, and the enmity between the two was ancient and deep-seated. But suddenly God's Spirit began to break out among this group of second-class Jews. The church at Jerusalem sent up Peter and John, their top leadership, and we wonder why. Was this the first rite of confirmation in which the bishops arrived to lay hands upon the new Christians? Or, did they come because the Samaritans had been considered so inferior in the eyes of the Jews that it was particularly important to put the official seal of approval on these new converts? John was the disciple who had earlier wanted to send fire and brimstone down upon these people because they were unworthy. That same John now came to call them brothers and sisters and confirm that all those who call Jesus Lord are one.

This first evangelistic effort in Samaria raises a lot of questions we are still dealing with as a church. The whole idea of evangelism remains controversial. I was thinking recently about the angel choir God commissioned on that first Christmas Eve to sing to the shepherds. Let's suppose they had a little meeting beforehand and began to raise all the usual anti-evangelism arguments. "Now wait a minute. What are we doing here? We're supposed to sing to these poor shepherds, and yet they all have their own values. They have their own way of worship. Who are we to disturb their priorities? Let's think it over. Would it be kind? Would it be tactful?" We can imagine those who prevailed saying, "Wait a minute. We've got the greatest news the world has ever heard—news they've been waiting for. We're going to sing. We're going to disturb all their values with the Good News." You and I are called to be angel choruses, going out and singing that same Good News.

Scene three is set in Gaza. Illogical priorities crop up again. Philip is the Billy Graham of his time. He is the kingpin, the center, the one through whom marvelous things are happening by the power of God. In the midst of this revival, the angel directs him, "Go down to a desert road." Immediately Philip goes. We might ask, "Why?" What would make someone leave a successful ministry with great crowds in order to meet and reach one insignificant person on a desert highway? That's the mystery of the church—her illogical priorities. Looking back, we can see the wisdom of the move. The Ethiopian was head of a large empire. Perhaps he was the means by which the gospel spread to Africa. But Philip had no way of knowing who would be traveling down the road. He was simply obedient.

The church continues to operate on seemingly illogical priorities. The size of the work is not the question. The issue is: where and to what is the Spirit leading us? As Americans, we are trained to think that every move must be upward to bigger and better things. Henri Nouwen, author of *The Wounded Healer* and other books, a Roman Catholic philosopher, left Yale University and all the contacts he had there to become the assistant priest in a tiny, impoverished parish in South America. He writes: "This downward mobility is unnatural for us because it belongs to the essence of our sinful, broken condition, that every fibre of our being is tainted by rivalry and competition. We're always finding ourselves, even against our own best desires and judgments, on the familiar road of upward mobility. The moment we think we are humble, we discover that we are wondering if we are more humble than our neighbor, and that we already have some type of reward in the back of our mind."

Like Philip, Christians are still acting from illogical priorities as they try to find God's direction. Recently a member of our congregation left a prestigious and well-paying job to do housework and baby-sitting for a year or two. She felt that God was calling her to change her priorities. The key is to believe that where you live and work and go to school, there are people as prepared for the Good News as the Ethiopian was, people who are dying to know

there is a way out of their trap and that God loves them. Karl
Marx's daughter, who was raised without religion, eventually became a Christian. In explaining how it happened, she said, "I
found this old German prayer and I thought, 'If there's a God like
that, I could believe in Him. . . .'" What was the prayer? It was
the Lord's Prayer, "Our Father, who art in heaven. . . ." Those
familiar words had fresh impact in the life of someone who was
ready.

Philip models for us what an evangelist does. He ministered to
the many and he went out to seek the one. Later on we find him an
evangelist in his own home, training new Christians there. We are
all called as well to be evangelists, like Philip. We are to find those
people whom God has prepared. We are to re-sort our own priorities, logical or illogical, and go and share the Good News.

CHAPTER TEN

How to Become a Christian

ACTS 9

One of my most profound desires for our nation is renewal, a renewal of God's Spirit moving through His
people. Beyond that I pray that that moving of the Spirit will result
in the renewal of every institution in our land, our land with so
much potential to serve God and be His people at this time in
history.

One of the great books of our time is John Gardner's *Self-
Renewal*, written about fifteen years ago, when he was Secretary of
Health, Education and Welfare in the President's cabinet.
Gardner later went on to found Common Cause. In this book he
says renewal is the only hope for survival for any organism: for
ourselves, our family, or any institution. Unless we go back to our
basic purpose and rediscover what it is we're meant to be, we are
destined to be like those dinosaurs who, in spite of their huge size,
finally died because their basic purpose was lost.

I hope for a renewal in our business community. If we can go back to our basic purpose, perhaps we can build better and cheaper cars than those competitors across the Pacific. That will only happen when labor and management can discover the satisfaction of working together to turn out a product that you and I as consumers are happy to buy. That's the key to the success of any business. I hope for renewal in our health care system, with hospitals once again focusing on the needs of their patients rather than on the convenience of the staff and relying less on the indiscriminate use of technology. I hope for renewal of the legal system in which cheap, equitable and rapid solutions of disputes are possible. I hope for renewal of education and government.

If the essence of renewal is to reexamine basic purposes, then what about the church of Jesus Christ? What does it mean for us to become what we're meant to be? What is our basic purpose? Obviously, it is not to build more stately mansions, even those great and inspiring cathedrals of Europe. It's not stewardship or even missions. It's not primarily feeding the poor and healing the sick, nor agitating for peace in our time, though these are all essential to the work of the church. The church's basic job is to produce and reproduce Christians. If we are doing that, all else follows. Those Christians then will feed the hungry and care for the poor and promote peace. They are to be faithful stewards and missionaries. Our basic job in this institution is to produce and reproduce Christians.

In writing about the gathering of the early church, Luke tells us that "the Lord added daily those who were being saved." That's normal and basic Christianity. Perhaps we need a clearer definition of a Christian. We'd like to think of a Christian as somebody who is good and kind and honest, but that's not necessarily so. We tend to think that being a Christian is synonymous with being religious. I would say that it is possible to be religious in the sense of observing all the forms, but not necessarily be a Christian. A Christian need not even be spiritual. If that's your predisposition, fine. But God loves and uses practical, pragmatic, unspiritual types just as much. A Christian is not necessarily theologically oriented, one who understands the mysteries of God. Such people are an asset to any congregation, but you can be theologically unsophisticated and be one of the great saints.

What, then, is a Christian? In the eighth chapter of Acts we have an account of one person becoming a Christian, and Luke, the writer, gives us, incidentally, two implicit definitions of the Christian. First of all, Saul has been given orders to go to Damascus and arrest "followers of the way." This is one of the earliest definitions of a Christian—a follower of the way. And that way is Jesus. He says in John 14:6, "I am the way, and the truth, and the life." In that first century, we were known as followers of the way, and it's an apt definition still. We are followers of Jesus and companions of His way.

The second definition of a Christian comes from verse 13. Ananias, in his prayer, speaks about the saints in Jerusalem. One primary definition is that a Christian is a saint. That does not mean that, as Christians, we are perfect or that there is a statue erected to us in some church. Saint means holy one—one who is set apart. A Christian is a saint, set apart for the work of Jesus Christ that He might do His work in and through us at our job, in our school, and in our neighborhood. The Christian is, according to this portion of Acts, a follower of the way and a saint.

From the biblical point of view, truth is a person. Truth is not a concept we learn or an ethical code we follow. Truth is a person named Jesus. Further, faith ought to be considered a verb. In faith, we commit ourselves to the way, to the person, to the Lord. We can't promise to be good. We can only say, "Lord, here I am, take me and make me Your servant." We become a saint by a commitment of our will and we are set apart.

Becoming a Christian, we enter into a relationship not unlike the relationship of marriage. It doesn't matter how or when we got married. It doesn't matter if the courtship was sudden or gradual. At a specific point in time, we changed status legally. For some people this is preceded by a dramatic, lights-flashing, bells-ringing experience, but this is irrelevant to our now being married. We could compare the whole experience to crossing a river. One can cross the mighty Mississippi at the widest part at flood tide and be a hero. On the other hand, at a certain place in Minnesota where the Mississippi begins, one can step across it. It doesn't matter where we cross the river at the easiest place or the hardest place; the point is, there is no doubt about whether or not we have crossed it.

The same can be said of being a Christian. How good a Christian you are is not the issue biblically. How good a spouse are you in your marriage? If I asked you if you're married you wouldn't say, "Well, I'm trying," or, "I'm reading some good books," or, "You know, some days I really think I'm married and then some days I know I'm not." Marriage is a relationship that begins at some specific point in time, and you would answer my question with a yes or a no. We can have the same certainty about being Christians. Being a Christian has nothing to do with being perfect, or living a problem-free life. You begin a relationship with somebody who becomes your Lord.

Becoming a Christian is the great watershed in life. Paul refers to this watershed on four separate occasions. It was the experience that changed his life. He tells the story twice in the Book of Acts, once before the king and again before an angry mob threatening to lynch him. He says, "Just a minute. Let me tell you about my conversion." It's a watershed moment in our lives as well. Whether we have come to that watershed suddenly or gradually, calmly or emotionally is incidental.

Sometimes we are put off by the words used to describe the experience, like "born again" and "converted" or "Spirit-filled," but such terms can be limiting. Jesus used the phrase "born again" with one person on one occasion. Basically, a Christian is a follower of the way and a saint set apart for God's purposes, and that requires an act of the will. If you're planning to be married you have many options in terms of the structure, length, content, and location of the ceremony. In the same way, there are as many ways to find God as there are people. In this ninth chapter of Acts we find a pattern that God seems to use often in order to bring us up to and beyond this watershed experience of becoming a Christian.

First of all, God gets our attention through a model. In Saul's case, it was Stephen. Stephen, the first deacon, was a man full of wisdom and power and grace, who cared for the poor. Stephen was stoned to death and Saul was present, "consenting to his death." Saul watched this one he had unjustly condemned being stoned and dying nobly, filled with love and grace. Stephen represents the person in your life who holds up a Christian commitment and life style you can't explain. He demonstrated courage and love for his persecutors, even while he was being stoned. Saul watched as the stones were hurled and heard Stephen say, "Lord, forgive them. Lay it not against them." I'm sure Saul watched in amazement, unable to account for this singular behavior.

God may have sent someone like that to you in your office, your school or your neighborhood. Even though that person may have our same problems and misfortunes, he or she somehow seems to have resources beyond human explanation. God uses such people to get our attention. Long before you were aware of God, He may have sent a Stephen into your life. We want the resources we see in such a person. We're like the lady who went to her doctor and said, "Doctor, I know I've been working too hard, but I don't want you to tell me to stop burning the candle at both ends. What I need is more wax." Most of us have been in that spot, needing more wax to live by, and God sends someone like Stephen into our lives, someone in whom rivers of living waters are flowing. We are intrigued and envious. We want what they have.

I read recently about Malcolm Muggeridge's conversion. At age 79, this British atheist found the Lord and joined the Roman Catholic Church. Asked to explain his conversion, Muggeridge said he could resist all the great books and all the great sermons. But when he saw Mother Teresa in Calcutta with the poor, he said, "If this is it, I've got to have it." She was the Stephen in Malcolm Muggeridge's life. In her was an artesian well of the Spirit which caught his attention.

In my infantry company in World War II, I met a Stephen. He was our chaplain. He didn't smoke or drink. He knew his Bible. He loved the Lord and he talked about Him a lot. There weren't many chaplains like him in those chaotic days. He was indefatigable in caring for others and preaching the Word, and I could not dismiss his witness. He proved to be the Stephen of my life. Bishop Fulton Sheen once said: "There are only two classes of people in all the world, those who have found God and those who are looking for Him, and everybody is looking, thirsting, hungry, seeking, and the great sinners are closer than the proud intellectuals. God prefers a loving sinner to a loveless saint."

The second person essential to Saul's watershed experience was Ananias. On the Damascus Road, Saul meets the risen Christ face to face. Few of us have had that experience. He hears a voice calling him by name. But that is not when he is converted. The immediate result is that he catches something like the flu. He is blind, with scales over his eyes, and he can't eat or sleep. He has met Jesus, but he is sick and miserable. In the surprising question of verse 4, "Saul, Saul, why do you persecute *me?*" Jesus is really telling Saul that because He lives in us, His Spirit dwells in us, and in persecuting Christians, Saul is persecuting Him. Saul is decimated, physically and emotionally, because he has been opposing God so zealously all these years.

He continues into Damascus a broken man, sick and blinded, and he stays that way until Ananias comes into his life. Ananias might have been a sandal-maker, but whatever his occupation, he was a devout and faithful follower of the way. He comes to pray with Saul and to provide the turning point in his life. Ananias says to this murderer of Christians, "Brother Saul." He greets him as a fellow Christian and puts his arms around him and prays with him. Suddenly the scales fall from Paul's eyes. He is healed and he is baptized.

I was not a very good student of biology, but one thing I remember well is the theory of mitosis—that all life must come from previously existing life. Life doesn't just happen in a vacuum. Cells have to divide. We can only become grandparents as our children have children. This is how life is passed on. The same thing is true in the spiritual world. Jesus tells us that the keys of the kingdom are in our hands. When Ananias calls on someone who is sick with spiritual flu, a physical transmission of the Spirit takes place. It sounds strange and mysterious, I know, but I'm convinced Ananias had to be present physically to act as an agent through whom spiritual cell division took place.

In his watershed experience, Saul simply calls Jesus Lord. He becomes His servant—a follower of the way and a saint. It seems to me we have made too much of the phrase "accepting Christ as your Savior." There's no power in knowing that Jesus died for the sins of the world, and for your sins; the devil, who understands all things, knows that. But he's not a Christian or a follower of the way. We become Christians when we call the Savior of the world "Lord." In saying that, we put our lives under new management. We ask Him to help us to be what He wants, and to do what He wants.

Ananias's role was relatively simple. He went to Saul's house and said, "The Lord, Jesus, sent me." He laid hands on Saul and Saul became Paul the Apostle. Ananias didn't need a course in evangelism to do that, and neither do we. The Lord can send us to someone who has spiritual flu, or somebody who is fed up with the chaos of his or her life. All we need to say is, "Have you had enough? Do you want Jesus to be Lord of your life?" That's the Ananias ministry that's open to all of us.

Some of you may be familiar with the story of Gert Behanna, one of the great evangelists of fifteen or twenty years ago. Gert was a wealthy, overprivileged, Waldorf Astoria–raised hothouse flower. She married three times and divorced three times. She was an alcoholic, on dope, and suicidal. One day, when she was in her fifties, she was at a dinner party in Connecticut, sitting next to a couple of new Christians, Tom and Blanche Page. During dinner, in an attempt to shock these Christians, she told her life's story, how bad she was, what a mess she was. When she finally wound down, Tom, an advertising executive, turned to her and said, "Gert, you've had a tough life. Why don't you just turn it over to the Lord?" Gert was indignant. "What? You mean like asking a redcap to take my bags?" He said, "Exactly." Gert considered the whole concept disgusting.

The next day she returned to her home in Lake Forest, Illinois, relieved to be rid of these strange people. But Tom and Blanche wrote to her, sent her some books, and added that they were praying for her. In a matter of days, she found herself kneeling beside her bed saying, "Lord, take all the bags I've been carrying, my life, the whole thing," and He did. Gert Behanna went on to write *The Late Liz*, a book that sold a million copies, and spent the remaining years of her life traveling up and down this land as an evangelist. Tom Page had proved to be the Ananias of her life.

The Swiss physician Paul Tournier tells about an experience he had after writing his first book. He went back to his medical school to visit his favorite old professor and asked for an afternoon of his time. As they sat in the gathering gloom of a Swiss winter afternoon, Paul read his new book to his old teacher. When he finished, he looked up to find tears in the old man's eyes. "Oh, Paul," he said, "that's a wonderful book. Everyone of us Christians should read that." Tournier was surprised. "I didn't know you were a Christian, professor. When did you become one?" "Just now, as you read your book." Paul was the Ananias for his beloved old teacher.

Chapter 9 of Acts goes on to tell us what life was like for the new Christian Saul. He immediately became a witness to Jesus. He didn't go to seminary or take any courses. If you have met the Lord of life, who has changed your life, you are equipped to tell others about that experience. Paul grew in both wisdom and power and he faced pressure, problems and persecution as he lived out his faith. Nevertheless, he was understandably viewed with suspicion by the Christians in Jerusalem because of his past activities, and that was when a third pivotal person came on the scene.

The same Barnabas we read about earlier, who sold a field and contributed the proceeds to the apostles, took Saul under his wing. He intervened for him with those in power. Many of us can attribute our spiritual maturity to a Barnabas in our lives—that person who took us to our first prayer group or urged us to join a class or serve on a committee—someone who introduced us to the larger fellowship. Barnabas simply was a friend who came alongside. Paul might not have been fully accepted as a new Christian and eventually as an apostle, except for Barnabas. I thank God for the Barnabases in my own life and in the lives of so many fellow Christians, the men and women who befriend, disciple, and affirm those new in the faith.

I think God wants us to emulate all three of the saints He used so mightily in Paul's life. We are to be Stephen, full of God's grace and love, even in adversity. We are to be Ananias, coming at the right time to someone with spiritual flu, praying with that person and passing on God's life to him or her. We are to be Barnabas, sons and daughters of encouragement, coming alongside new Christians to shepherd and guide.

Our daughter and her husband, who live in Florida, recently bought four chickens. The plan was to have fresh eggs every morning. Six months later, there were still no eggs. I said, "Chris, go out and tell those hens, 'It's either eggs or fried chicken.'" She is more patient than that, and besides, she loves those chickens. But the point is that chickens are meant to lay eggs. Christians are meant to reproduce Christians, and God may be giving you a chance to do that one of these days.

Finally, for those who are still wrestling with how to become a Christian, let me remind you of something Lloyd George once said: "Don't be afraid to take a big step if one is indicated. You can't cross a chasm in two small jumps." To become a Christian we need only decide to put our lives under new management and take that jump.

CHAPTER ELEVEN

Life: Waiting or Journey?

ACTS 10, 11

An optometrist I know has a sign in his office that reads, "If you don't see what you're looking for, you've come to the right place." When Barnabas was sent by the church at Jerusalem to check out the new Christian church at Antioch, we don't know what he was looking for. But we read in the eleventh chapter of Acts about what he saw. He saw the grace of God and was glad. I wonder, what was it exactly that he saw? How do we see the grace of God? How do we see the wind of God's power and the fire of His presence?

One answer is found in the marvelous verses in Colossians 1:26–27, where Paul talks about "the mystery hidden for ages and generations but now made manifest to you all. To them God chose to make known how great among the Gentiles are the riches of the glory of this mystery, which is Christ in you, the hope of glory." Barnabas saw a roomful of Christians just like us, men and women in whom Christ dwelt, and he saw the wind and the fire, God's presence and power, and was glad.

In chapters 10 and 11 of Acts, we find the beginning of a crosscultural gospel. For the first time, those totally outside the Jewish camp are converted. You will remember that the Ethiopian eunuch was already somewhat of a convert to Judaism when Philip found him reading Old Testament Scriptures. The Samaritans were half-breed Jews. But now for the first time Gentiles, those absolutely outside the Jewish race, accept the Christian faith. Cornelius, the Roman soldier, is the first of many. He is the spiritual ancestor of all of us who are not genetically Jewish. God has prepared him through his prayers, his goodness, and his hopes. At the same time, God works at the other end of the spectrum and deals with Peter. Through a dream his mind is emptied of all preconceptions of what is clean and unclean. Peter, being prepared, trusts God and goes to the house of the Gentile Cornelius. The same process of spiritual cell division occurs which we spoke of earlier. Peter finds a prepared person, and the Holy Spirit comes to dwell in the first Gentile and his family.

Isn't it remarkable that the Gospel found its way to the Gentiles simply because of the persecution of the early Christians! They fled Jerusalem in order to save their lives and, incidentally, brought the Gospel all around that part of the Mediterranean world. They began by preaching mainly to other Jews. However, in Antioch, the Greeks heard and responded and a church was born—a purely Gentile church, a powerful center for disseminating the Gospel of Jesus Christ.

When Cornelius and his household become Christians, the Jerusalem church reacts with typical caution. When they learn that a whole host of non-Jews in Antioch have accepted Jesus as Lord, they decide to send someone to investigate all this firsthand. They send Barnabas, one of their most valuable and trusted leaders. He sees the grace of God and knows there has been an effective work of the Spirit. Sensing that this church needs the wisdom and theology of Paul, he recruits his friend and teammate, and together they lay the foundation there for a mighty church, a church with a history of sending missionaries and giving alms and claiming the world for Jesus. That ministry begins almost immediately when they hear that a famine is expected in Jerusalem. They

arrange to take up an offering and send it on to their spiritual
family in the parent church.

It seems to me there is an important distinction between these
two churches, the Jerusalem church and the Antioch church. The
Jerusalem church is cautious and conservative, concerned for
right doctrine and fearful of moving out boldly. It is a static
church, waiting for something, perhaps the second coming. On
the other hand, the Antioch church is on a journey. It is moving
out—claiming, sending, and giving. The Jerusalem church is
concerned with tradition while the Antioch church is at the center
of innovation. The Jerusalem church is a church that reacts. The
Antioch church is one that proacts. The contrast is between the
conservative and innovative, the cautious and the daring. In historical perspective, we see the center of the Christian church
moving from its roots at Jerusalem to Antioch and thus to the rest
of the Greek and Roman world.

We have likened God's Spirit in the church to wind and fire,
and there are different ways of handling wind and fire. We can say,
"The wind is up; let's reef the sails lest we tip over." This is what
the Jerusalem church seemed to do. Or, we can say, "The wind is
up, let's put on all the canvas we've got," as they did in Antioch.
When the fire of God's presence was felt, the Jerusalem church
was cautious. "Let's bank the fires, lest they get out of hand." In
Antioch, apparently they said, "Get the bellows. Blow on it. Let's
make it burn."

It seems to me the church is still faced with the choice between
these two different life styles. We can *react* to the horrors around
us, for example, of nuclear war, and become survivalists. We can
say that destruction is inevitable and build shelters to save ourselves. Or, we can become peacemakers. We can *proact*. What is
our stance in the face of declining membership of the main line
churches? We can say, "Ain't it awful? The Spirit is leaving the
church." Or, we can move out boldly in the sure knowledge that
the world is hungry for the Good News. When the moment of
opportunity comes and a Cornelius has been prepared, we're on
the scene to transmit life and the Good News.

Years ago, the World Council of Churches had their first meeting in Amsterdam. Stephen Neil, a bishop in India, spoke on evangelism to a churchful of bishops and church leaders. He said, "I want to ask you bishops and church leaders how long it has been since you, personally, introduced someone to Jesus Christ." He knew that when the bishops and church leaders start doing that, the laity will also. That's called leadership by modeling, and it works!

The church's role goes far beyond reacting to and opposing all the terrible things that are happening in the world. We can too easily find ourselves in the role of the villagers the Greek poet C. P. Cavafy wrote about in his poem, "Waiting for the Barbarians." It begins:

> What are we waiting for, packed in the Forum?
> The Barbarians are due here today.
> Why isn't anything going on in the Senate?
> Why have the senators given up legislating?
> Because the Barbarians are coming today.
> What's the point of senators and their laws now?
> When the Barbarians get here, they'll do the legislating.
> Why did our Emperor set out so early to sit on the throne at the
>   city's main gate, in state, wearing the crown?
> Because the Barbarians are coming today and the Emperor is
>   waiting to receive their leader.
> He's even got a citation to give him, loaded with titles and
>   imposing names.

The poem goes on to set the stage of a city paralyzed by the horrors to come. But it ends this way:

> Why this sudden bewilderment, this confusion?
> (How serious everyone looks!)
> Why are the streets and the squares rapidly emptying,
> everyone going home so lost in thought?
> Because it's night and the Barbarians haven't come.
> And some people just in from the border say
> 'There are no Barbarians any longer.'

Now what's going to happen to us without them? The Barbarians
were a kind of solution.

As a church we can spend our efforts reacting to all the problems
around us—corruption, pornography and the rest, or we can proact like the church at Antioch, with a message of hope for the
world. Instead of carefully checking out the orthodoxy of every
new thing, we can begin to make new things happen. The church
at Antioch could not have come into being at a worse time historically and strategically. The Romans were persecuting the Christians. The Jews were violently opposed to this new sect called
Christians, or followers of the way. The democracy of Greece had
been destroyed. The Roman Empire was in collapse. Immorality
was everywhere. It seemed the worst of all possible times and yet
the Christians were a people with a vision. They worked hard,
preached the Gospel diligently and cared for the needy of the
world, so much so that in about three hundred years, the year 312
to be exact, Constantine, the emperor of Rome, declared Rome a
Christian empire. That mighty movement had its start at Antioch,
where the church took on the whole world and finally won.

On a more personal level, it seems to me we can choose to be
either Jerusalem Christians or Antioch Christians. I read recently
that actuarial tables say that a sixty-year-old, standard issue, white,
nonsmoking, American male has a life expectancy of 21.6 addi-
tional years. But such a statistic is absolutely meaningless personally. I could die tomorrow, or I could live twenty years beyond the
actuarial tables. The tables tell us how long we will live if we're
average, but obviously, very few of us are average, and beyond
that, the length of our life is not the issue. Whether you're twenty,
forty, sixty, or eighty, what will you do with the time you have left?
God must give you a vision for your life. A church full of people
with such a vision for what God wants and expects, and empowers
them to be and do, is a church in the Antioch tradition.

CHAPTER TWELVE

Angel Talk

ACTS 12

Communicating is one of the major challenges that you
and I face every day. In marriage, most conflict comes
because we don't really understand what our partner is trying to
say. At every level we have problems and divisions because communication is so difficult. I heard about a small business that
received a request from some government agency asking them to
list all of their employees broken down by sex. The reply came
back, "None! Our problem is absenteeism."

I think we need to communicate more clearly on the subject of
angels. As Christians, our beliefs in and about angels are varied.
Some would say, "I believe in them. I think I met one once."
Others would say, "That's a side issue. We are here to serve Jesus.
That's spooky stuff." Any discussion about angels could create very
natural divisions.

I'd like to raise three questions in regard to angels that the
twelfth chapter of Acts helps us answer. First of all, are there
angels, real angels? I don't mean Hell's Angels or the Guardian

Angels who patrol areas in major cities where people are constantly victimized by crime. I'm not speaking about the angel Moroni, whose great statue sits on top of Mormon temples. I'm talking about real angels, and according to the Bible, they exist. Scripture gives us many accounts of some sort of sinless beings who serve God and intervene in the affairs of men. In the Old Testament, Isaiah reports God saying to Jerusalem, "I have put silent, never-sleeping watchmen all around the city."

The next question is, what are they like? The biblical evidence seems to indicate they are male, since they are always referred to as "he." It tells us they are sinless and that they serve God in specific tasks, and apparently they are often unrecognizable and without credibility. When Peter is confronted by this miraculous being in prison, he has trouble believing the whole thing is real. When he is finally outside, he is forced to conclude that this must have been an angel. That gives us one test by which we discern a genuine angel. Do they help God's people accomplish His work?

Assuming then that there are angels, what is their purpose? What can we expect of them? Literature is full of authentic saints, both ancient and contemporary, who report that they have met someone who seems to be an angel. Festo Kivengere, a Ugandan bishop, tells of fleeing with his family from Idi Amin and crossing the African plains by night to Kenya. I have been to Africa, and I can attest that nothing is darker than night on the African plain. The Kivengere family became seriously lost three different times, and on all three occasions, a man appeared to them to point them in the right direction. By dawn they arrived safely at their destination. Kivengere can't say with certainty that these were angels, but someone appeared miraculously to preserve one of God's special servants and his family.

Another contemporary saint with a similar experience is an Indian named Sadhu Sundarsingh, a legendary evangelist in India and throughout Asia. He tells about preaching in Tibet and offending the chief lama by his proclamation of the gospel. He was thrown down a well; the lid was sealed with a great cover and locked, and he was left to die. In the fall, his left arm was injured seriously, and he fell among the bones and rotting flesh of others who had been imprisoned in the same well. For the next three days and nights he prayed constantly and cried out to God. On the third night, he says that the door of the well suddenly opened. A rope was lowered, fortunately with a loop in it, because he was unable to hang on. He put his foot in and one arm, and he was pulled up. He got out of the well to find no one there. He slept that night and in the morning went back to the same village and again began preaching Jesus. The chief lama was enraged and set out to find out who had helped him escape. The subsequent investigation proved that the only key to the lid of the well rested on the belt of the chief lama. Again, Sundarsingh could not say with certainty that he was rescued by angels. But there seems to be no logical explanation for his miraculous delivery.

Hope McDonald, wife of one of our Presbyterian pastors here in Seattle, has just written a book entitled *When Angels Appear*. She has traveled around the country interviewing any number of people who claim to have seen angels. Years ago I heard the story of a neurologist in Philadelphia, S. W. Mitchell, who tells about answering a knock on his door one blizzardy night. A little girl covered with sleet and snow was standing on the doorstep and saying, "Come help my mother. She is sick, and our phone is not working." The doctor got his coat and followed the little girl to a house several blocks away, where he found a woman seriously ill with pneumonia. He immediately called an ambulance and while they were waiting for it to arrive, he remarked, "I'm so glad your daughter had the wisdom to come and get me." The woman was baffled. "My daughter died a month ago," she said. "Her clothes are still in that closet over there." Examining the closet, the doctor found the very coat and dress the little girl had been wearing, warm and dry and obviously unused that stormy night. We are left wondering if that little girl was an angel. The good doctor is not sure.

I believe, in faith, that there are angels, though I have never seen one. Further, the Bible gives us a clear report on the kinds of things they say. In this twelfth chapter of Acts, the angel, first of all, kicks Peter to get his attention. (Is it hard to imagine an angel kicking you?) "Wake up," he says. "Get up. Put on your shoes and your belt. Put on your coat and follow me." He leads Peter out of the prison and promptly disappears. That's a sample of genuine angel talk. I don't think, contrary to popular belief, that angels say, "Glory, glory, hallelujah." They deal with the stuff of life—in Peter's case, what to do to get out of the mess he was in. Angels seem to deal in the real situations and problems of life.

When Peter is liberated, he goes to the home of Christians who are in the midst of a prayer meeting asking for his release and deliverance. Rhoda, the maid, answers his knock on the door. She is so excited that instead of admitting him, she runs inside to announce, "Peter is here." Had I written this part of the Bible, I would have had them respond, "Why, of course he's here. We've been praying for him and expecting him. What took him so long?"

That's not what the Scriptures say happened. The saints of the good old days are just about like the saints of today. They are so caught up in their prayers that they forget to believe. Unlike the angel, they are caught up in doing something spiritual. Angels are busy carrying out God's will. They haven't time to be spiritual. So often we Christians get sidetracked into being spiritual for its own sake. We so enjoy the prayer meetings that we forget the purpose of our prayers, which is that God's will be done in our lives. In any event, expected or not, God answered their prayers and Peter was delivered.

I think over the years one of the church's main problems has been an overemphasis on spirituality. We've been accused of being so spiritual that we are no earthly good. In January 1983, *Reader's Digest* published a serious attack on both the National Council of Churches and the World Council of Churches for their support of some somewhat questionable causes. The articles reopened the age-old but unnecessary debate of the church between the liberal social action group and the evangelical part who emphasize proclamation of the Kingdom of God.

Jesus began His ministry by saying that He was the fulfillment of the Old Testament Scripture claiming that, through Him, "the blind see, the deaf hear, the lame are healed, the poor have good news preached to them." These were His credentials, but not His mission. His mission was to proclaim the Kingdom and Himself as King. One part of the church accuses the rest of having no credentials. All they do is talk about the Kingdom. What about the poor, the lame, the oppressed, the homeless refugees, the threat of nuclear war? The other group replies that those are side issues and our primary mission is to proclaim the Kingdom. I believe we had better do both. We need to wed our spirituality to the practicality of the angels.

I read recently about a man named Homer Farmer from Sacramento, California, who is eighty plus and a former stockbroker. He has started something called "Homer's Army." It seems that when the harvesters go through the fields of all the vast farms in the area, hundreds of tons of food are left behind. Homer's Army, all of whose recruits are retirement age, moves in and gleans the thousands of tons of food remaining. They keep half for themselves and give the other half away to feed the hungry. Homer claims there is enough food left over in our fields to feed every hungry person in our nation and beyond. Here's what he says: "Gerontologists say that to have a really long life you need fresh air, sunshine, exercise, fresh food, and a reason for living. We have it all." Homer's revelation to get those senior citizens working to provide for themselves and others could be considered the kind of authentic angel talk we've been discussing—concrete directions concerning how we can bring about positive change and bless others.

Finally, we might ask what difference it all makes to believe that God has angels at His disposal, mysterious beings able to intervene and do His will. For me, such a belief assures me that God, through His Holy Spirit, is ultimately in charge of the church. Angels don't report to the elders or the board of deacons or even to bishops or popes. Angels report to God alone. When we mess things up on a human level, God has at His disposal beings who can intervene and change the course of affairs.

Second, angels remind us that there is no handbook for living the Christian life. You and I, as God's faithful people, must come to Him faithfully and regularly. I recommend that along with your daily prayers, you spend time listening to God. Use a pad and pencil to write down what you think God is saying. We need to be sensitive to the new thing God may be trying to do in our lives, to a new strategy. Our lives are not predictable. In the same time period when the Apostle James went to prison and was killed, the Apostle Peter was delivered safely from prison. On an earlier occasion, in Acts, Peter was released from prison only to go right back to the temple to preach Jesus. This time he went into hiding for his very life. You see, there is no one strategy for living the Christian life as a student, a businessman, or even a preacher. Rather, we need to live our lives attuned to God so that He might tell us what to do and be in this moment.

Perhaps the most important lesson we learn from this encounter of Peter and the angel is that we need to relax and trust God. If we are His persons and our lives are in His hands, then our commission is to trust Him. Our faith is not in the fact that we will be delivered. James wasn't and those martyrs fed to lions weren't. The fact is, if God wants us delivered in this life, we will be delivered. But that's His business. If He doesn't deliver us, we trust Him. If He does, we praise Him, and continue to trust Him.

I love the fact that Peter, on this night before he was to face certain execution, is sleeping so soundly that the angel can scarcely wake him up. Occasionally I wake up at four o'clock in the morning and can't go back to sleep. I realize I'm not trusting God. I say to myself, "What is the matter with you? Who is in charge of your life?" Sometimes, I still can't sleep, but the point is, if we really trust God, we ought to be sleeping well.

Dr. William Appleton, an assistant clinical professor of psychiatry at Harvard Medical School, tells us that researchers are discovering a new disease called "hurry sickness." Those who feel time is running out are suffering from this disease. You can have it at any age—eighteen, fifty-eight or ninety-eight. Dr. Appleton says, "It's a *major* cause of the entire range of chronic and degenerative diseases—including heart disease, ulcers, high blood pressure and possibly even cancer. People with 'hurry sickness,' as a group, get sick earlier and die earlier. They are susceptible to every type of stress-related ailment, because all illness is affected in some way by a person's sense of time." I think Dr. Appleton is onto something. John Wesley once said, "I have no time to be in a hurry." If you trust God, you believe that there is enough time in every day to do God's will in that day. We can be like Peter and sleep soundly in the midst of a life-threatening situation.

Years ago I saw a sign in a psychiatrist's office which said: "In two days tomorrow will be yesterday." That's a healthy perspective, especially if we let God control today and tomorrow as well as yesterday.

As we said earlier, angels are sinless beings who serve God. Herod, in this twelfth chapter of Acts, embodies the very opposite of that. King Herod was a sinful man who served himself. He was full of his own importance. I heard about a woman who was celebrating her thirtieth anniversary and who was asked, "To what do you attribute the success of your long marriage?" "That's easy," was the reply. "We have so much in common. My husband and I have been in love with the same man for thirty years." To be in love with yourself, totally preoccupied with your own concerns, is what sin is all about. That was Herod's problem. The Scripture here tells us he glorified himself, not God, and he was smitten by an angel, eaten by worms, and he died.

I heard of a salesman who was called into his sales manager's office, on the wall of which was a big map full of pins indicating the deployment of the firm's salesmen all over the country. "Now, Cartright," said the sales manager, "I want you to understand the gravity of your situation. I'm not going to fire you, but I am going to loosen your pin a little bit." If the primary people in your life are loosening your pin a little bit, start praying and trusting. Our job is to pray believing. "The prayer of a righteous man has great power in its effects" (James 5:16). Let us believe that as we pray, God might be dispensing an angel to accomplish His will in our life just as He did with Peter. The door of our prison may mysteriously open and we may be delivered from the "insurmountable" problems we are facing this day and this week.

CHAPTER THIRTEEN

God in History

ACTS 13

In the twelve years I worked in New York City, I discovered one of that city's great vehicles of communication—the graffiti on subway walls. Much is obscene, but some is profound. On one occasion, the New York Bible Society featured a poster on which was written the verse "The meek shall inherit the earth." In felt-tip pen below that, some sage had written, "We don't want it!" All of which brings up the question of our view of the world: in the light of past history, where is the world headed?

Each of us interprets history differently. If you were to tell me your view of history, I would know a great deal about you. Our many divisions, philosophical and religious, are often the result of our differing views of history. You may believe in a cyclical view in which the same events and conditions, war and peace, famine and prosperity, continue in never-ending cycles. You may believe that life moves along with no special meaning and that events, benign or catastrophic, simply happen. You may believe that we are here marking time, waiting for some much larger cosmic event to take place. We Christians have a very definite and specific view of history. We believe that God is in history, that He is working in history, and that He can use us as instruments in that history.

One summer my wife and I spent my study leave in a very tiny village which, nevertheless, had three Protestant churches. On three successive Sundays, we attended each of them. In the first church, we were made very much aware of the world scene. The sermon, prayers, and announcements all emphasized their concern for countries and causes beyond that town and that sanctuary. The injustices of the world were prayed for and preached about. That congregation had an inclusive world-view. The second church was just next door, and we worshiped there a week later. The service ran for over two hours. They had a snare drum in the chancel and other musicians playing guitars and tambourines. We really enjoyed their freedom and spontaneity, but nothing was preached about or prayed for outside of the experience of the worshipers in that sanctuary. Their concern was entirely focused on themselves and their church and their own needs. On the third Sunday we attended a "biblical" church. We heard about nothing in song, preaching, or prayers that didn't take place two thousand or more years ago.

If you were to ask me which of those churches I felt more comfortable in, I'd have to say, "None." I don't want to have to choose between a personal God who cares about every need or a global God calling us to action in the world, or a God who acted dramatically in history two thousand years ago. What we are as a church reflects our belief about history, and about an omnipotent God who is architect of that history. History from the Christian perspective is dynamic and unpredictable. One way in which we differ from all the animals, all created things, is that we alone are unfinished creatures. Every other creature is complete. An eagle is an eagle, a rabbit a rabbit, an elephant an elephant, expected to be nothing more, nothing less. Only we humans are unfinished in terms of our personhood, offered multiple choices at each stage of development. Our corporate history is also incomplete, and we can choose what we will become. To say this may sound like heresy, but I suspect that God is still working out His designs in history, and that we, His products, reflect that "work-in-progress" concept.

The thirteenth chapter of the Book of Acts deals specifically with God's interaction and intervention in history. We discover that He is a *personal* God. The first great missionary journey of the church began so inconspicuously. Two people started off, traveled down to the seacoast, and booked passage to Cyprus. They began with no special fanfare, yet the course of history was changed because of that first missionary journey carrying the Good News from Antioch to Rome and the whole civilized world. The Holy Spirit spoke to the Christians as they were worshiping and directed them to "set aside Paul and Barnabas" and send them. They were not told to appoint a committee, but to send out two particular people. The two men were not elected. They were chosen by God through His Holy Spirit.

I believe this is still a valid way to find leadership in the church. We are not elders or deacons or preachers or teachers through our own choosing, but because God has called us. He chooses us for specific tasks. Ordination or the laying on of hands does not confer power. It confirms and recognizes God's own call. Simeon saw the power of the Holy Spirit to heal and he wanted to buy this powerful gift. He was rebuked. This kind of power is not for sale. Only God can give it.

We recognize, then, that God is personal, but He is also *political*. There are significant people at every level in life who are key people, those who are the hinges upon whom great doors may swing. As these missionaries moved out into Cyprus, God used them to get the attention of the proconsul, the governor of Cyprus. Suddenly a very key person became a friend of the faith. In terms of the Kingdom, that was an excellent political move. We see this same sense of the political in the conversion of the Ethiopian eunuch. He was a highly placed person in the queen's court. The first Gentile convert, Cornelius, was a strategically placed Roman officer. God's strategy does not ignore the political, and you and I must not discount it either.

Not only is God in the personal and the political, but He is also in the *process* of history. When Paul and Barnabas arrived in Antioch of Pisidia, Paul spoke in the synagogue and described God's actions in history. I love all the action verbs he used. God *chose*, He *led*, He *bore with*, He *destroyed*, He *gave*, He *raised up*. Paul made it clear that God's hand is demonstrated in history. Our belief as Christians that God is the architect of this dynamic history separates us from most religions. For the most part, they believe that somewhere along the way the world and everything in it was created by some God, some force, and that we will someday return in some form to that primal state. Only Christians believe that history is dynamic, changing, moving forward, and that it reflects the will and design of the God whom we worship.

I was on a trip recently with a noted American rabbi and at one point we were sitting together on a bus at the end of a long and tiring journey. To make conversation, I decided to find out something about his ministry. I said, "Assuming the Lord gives you five more years of life, my friend, what is the biggest dream you have for your congregation or for the Jewish congregation in America? What would you like to devote your prayers and your life to?" The rabbi's face went blank and he sat silent for a long time. Finally, he turned to me and said, "You don't understand; it's very hard to be a Jew. If I can just be a good Jew until I die it will be enough." He seemed to lack any sense of hope that God could enter in and change the course of events. If this rabbi's reaction is typical, the Jewish faith, out of which all Christians have come, would seem to have lost its dynamic view of history.

You and I can fall into the same sense of hopelessness about history. Presbyterians emphasize predestination, but predestination does not mean *"Que será, será"* ["Whatever will be, will be"]. It is not fatalism, which assumes that everything is already settled or decided. Our fate is not locked up in the stars or the cards or some crystal ball with which someone can read our fortune and tell us what's going to happen. In terms of world or global history or our own personal life, we believe that the future is systemic, not linear. Our future is unpredictable because we worship a dynamic

God. The future will be what you and I decide it will be with His help. We are not locked into anything.

An authentic interpretation of predestination is found in verse 48 of chapter 13. After the Gentiles have heard the Good News from Paul and Barnabas, we read that "as many as were ordained to eternal life believed." Everyone is not open to the message. You talk to two friends at work about the Good News of God in your life and one says, "How can I find it?" The other says, "Ho hum." We cannot explain why one is prepared to believe. The Bible indicates that there are those who are preordained to believe. But while predestination plays a part in individual faith, it has nothing to do with our future or the history of the world. All of that, as we said, is dynamic. History is a process with God as the architect, and the future is unpredictable.

In Perga, before they arrived in Antioch of Pisidia, John Mark, who had been assisting Paul and Barnabas, left them. It's interesting to speculate why. It is strange that he would choose to return to Jerusalem in the middle of their journey. Though Paul finally forgave him for his desertion, he resented his actions for a long, long time. He felt John Mark had abandoned them. Barnabas, the encourager, was more charitable. We can hear him reasoning with Paul, "He's only a kid. Come on. Give him a second chance." Paul finally did.

There are a number of theories about John Mark's untimely departure. He might have been fearful. The journey ahead was difficult with the possibility of robbers on the road, plus a steep climb over the mountains to the next town. Another explanation is that he was homesick. He was still a young lad and he may have missed his mother. That's the sentimental view. Or, his leaving may have been a matter of politics. John Mark was a loyal friend and fan of Barnabas, and from this point on, the missionary journeys of Barnabas and Paul became the missionary journeys of Paul and Barnabas. Paul took top billing, and it is a credit to Barnabas's magnanimous spirit that he was willing to assume the second place, uncomplainingly and happily. But it's possible that John Mark couldn't accept that change quite so easily.

Finally, in this microcosm of God in history that we find in chapter 13, we must conclude that God uses the petty. God can even use our sins. Paul and Barnabas came to Antioch. They were asked to preach in the synagogue and within a week's time great crowds gathered to hear them. Other Jews, we are told, were filled with jealousy. These two strangers with their new gospel were getting greater results than they were having.

Because the Jews were jealous of the success of Paul and Barnabas, they stirred up devout women and the leading men of the city against them. In response to that rejection, Paul and Barnabas turned to the Gentiles and a great work opened among all the non-Jews. The two missionaries realized that God wanted them to be a light for the Gentiles, bringing them salvation. That great work continues to this day.

God can work through strange circumstances. We're in a time right now when some of our more liberal seminaries are doing an about-face. For the first time in my lifetime there are more preachers than there are churches. For the first time, even the smallest church has choices in hiring a pastor. We're in a time when God seems to have put in the heart of His people the desire for the proclamation of Jesus' Kingdom. The liberal seminaries are losing out. They are more and more aware that to survive they may have to preach and teach a more personal gospel. Last year one liberal seminary hired their first professor of evangelism. Another leading liberal seminary in our country recently sent a delegation to Gordon-Conwell Seminary, asking about their formula for attracting students who will be acceptable to today's churches.

What then can we say? God is in history and history is dynamic. Our personal future is wide open and the church's future is wide open. The history of America and the world is not determined. As Christians we can affect that future as we do at least four things:

1. Believe that God is in the affairs of state as well as the affairs of the church and your own life. As James Costen, 1982 Moderator of the United Presbyterian Church said, "Pray with your newspaper in one hand, your Bible in the other, and have ready access to the Congressional Record."

2. Look for God in the big and the small. He is at work in those situations we find in the headlines, but He is also there in the seemingly insignificant and unspectacular. He is working out His will in your family, your office, your school, your neighborhood.

3. Pray for our leaders in both church and government. Pray for our present-day Sergius Pauluses and Corneliuses and all the governors and presidents. Pray that they will be instruments of God's will.

4. Pray for your own particular mission. You are as much set apart for mission as Paul and Barnabas. They were sent on a missionary journey. Your missionary journey may be just across the street. You may go to the next town, the next state or across the world. Believe that God still calls us and sets us apart, and that He can change history through you.

CHAPTER FOURTEEN

The Ups and Downs of Life

ACTS 14, 15

How would you respond to the question, "What is the purpose of the church?" One primary answer is found in one of my favorite verses, John 10:10, where Jesus tells us that He came that we might have life. The Greek word used for "life" here is *zoē*, which means "life pressed down, heaped up and running over." The image made new sense to me as I stood in a market in rural Kenya last year with our local church's missionaries Denny and Jeanne Grindall. Our van had broken down next to a market where hundreds of people, mostly women, were selling dried beans and rice and corn, all stored in great burlap sacks. Each buyer brought his or her own container, some kind of a tin cup, and when a purchase was made, the vendors heaped their product into the can until it was literally overflowing. In Africa, goods are sold not by careful weights and measures but heaped up and running over, as Jesus wants His life in us to be.

The purpose of the church is to help us to live now and forever

that abundant life. I don't know of any two single chapters in the
Bible that are more specific about the problems of everyday living
than Acts 14 and 15. Certainly we must all deal with the fact that
life is both changing and changeless. Recently I read the Naisbitt
Report, in which one of our most popular futurologists describes
the seven megatrends that are in the process of changing the shape
of life in America. The most significant of these trends is, I suppose, that we are ceasing to be an industrial society. Production is
moving to the Third World, and it appears that the United States
will become instead an information-gathering society. The author
predicts that this change will be more drastic than our previous
move from an agricultural to an industrial society. But there are
some things that never change about human nature and life. Just
to illustrate my point, let me give you the following quotes and
their surprising sources.

"I'm in difficulty, both summer and winter, about my sal-
ary."—An Egyptian in 256 B.C.
"The first of June and nothing done by the Senate!"—Cicero,
38 B.C.
"Who has not seen with his own eyes the present spirit which
forces up the price of commodities to such a degree that human
language cannot find words to express the transaction?"—Diocle-
tian, A.D. 301
"Athletics have become professionalized."—Socrates, 402 B.C.

One purpose of the church is to teach us how to deal with both
the changeless and the changing. But perhaps much of our difficulty comes from our false expectations about life. We get some of
these expectations from sincere people in the church who promise
the victorious life and say that if you really believe in Jesus and are
filled with His Spirit, life will be one rosy glow after another. The
Bible never promoted that idea. Then there's the notorious Rever-
end Ike, who tells his many followers that if they'll just send him
their money in faith, they'll all drive Cadillacs and be pros-

perous—that God wants all of His people rich. Such undisguised avarice seems a long way from the biblical picture of life in Christ.

What can we learn, then, about life and the living of it from these fourteenth and fifteenth chapters of Acts? First of all, we learn that life is full of ups and downs, for the Christian and the non-Christian, for the godly and the sinner alike. Along with death and taxes, ups and downs are a certainty. Paul and Barnabas have come to Iconium and a revival breaks out. They remain for a long time, but eventually persecution begins again and they flee for their lives. They move on to Lystra and encounter a lame man, whom Paul miraculously heals. The crowds are flabbergasted and call them gods. Paul and Barnabas are horrified by such behavior, and they rend their clothes. It was the Jewish custom to tear your clothes in the presence of blasphemy. Paul and Barnabas protest that they are not gods, but they can barely prevent the crowd from offering sacrifices to them.

By contrast, in the events of the *very* next verse, which we assume occur minutes or hours later, Jews come from Iconium and turn these enthusiastic new believers into a hostile mob. They stone Paul and leave him for dead. Those are pretty extreme ups and downs—from being hailed as a god one minute to being stoned the next. With his usual resiliency, Paul recovers, goes right back to the city, finds Barnabas, and sets off again the very next day for Derbe. They return shortly to Antioch of Pisidia and we find Paul preaching that marvelous word, so timely here, that "through many tribulations we must enter the Kingdom of God" (v. 22). He warns that they will have tribulations as believers. They are not exempt.

Finally, they return to Antioch, the beloved home church which sent them out. They make a report on their journeys on the mighty works that God had done in Iconium, Derbe, Lystra, how He had "opened the door of faith to the Gentiles" (v. 27). But, right on the heels of this loving homecoming, we find opposition and criticism arising. Jews from Jerusalem, the old reactionary guard, are complaining because these new believers were not circumcised and insisting that in order to become Christians, they must first become Jews. In other words, they are saying to Paul and Barnabas, "You did it wrong."

You and I can really identify with Paul and Barnabas here. We all have our critics, those who say, "You should have done it my way." Or, "Next time, here's how to do it." Or, "Let me tell you out of my vast experience what you should have done." There is no shortage of people like that in your life or mine. A friend of mine who is a very creative writer does not like critics of any kind. He claims, "They're like eunuchs in the harem. They know how it's done. They see it done every day. But they can't do it." Paul and Barnabas have brought the gospel to Asia Minor, witnessed revival, converted the Gentiles, but at home they face the critics who have never left the city but want to instruct them on how they should have done it. The ups and downs of life.

In Jerusalem, Paul and Barnabas find support from the two most prominent apostles, James and Peter, who stand up and defend them. The church finally works out a compromise in which the new Gentile converts will at least observe some of the old dietary rules handed down by Moses. In harmony once more, Paul and Barnabas are sent back to Antioch.

Yet, in the very next paragraph, these two remarkable servants of God, this effective missionary pair, brothers in the Lord, have a falling-out. They are about to leave to visit all their new churches and new converts once again, and there is a heated argument about whether or not they should bring along John Mark. They separate in anger. I suppose there are few pains in life quite like a separation from a brother or sister in the Lord, one who has been your prayer partner, mentor, traveling companion, and friend. You may both still be believers, but because of past hurts or differences, you choose separate paths. Perhaps those broken relationships are our bitterest "downs" in life. They surely have been for me.

None of us is protected from those "downs," large or small. You're president of your company with a corner office, a key to the executive washroom and a limousine at your disposal. Your stockholders vote a merger and since yours is the smaller company, you're jobless within a week. You're a teacher with tenure and enrollment drops off and you are no longer needed. You're a pastor under the impression that you're doing well, and your congregation decides to vote you out. You're married and you go off to work one morning, unaware of any impending trouble, and return that night to face a broken relationship, perhaps even a divorce. You've taken your good health for granted when suddenly a tumor appears and your life is threatened. We are living in a time when whole industries are closing down. We read in the papers that steel may no longer be a viable industry here in America, and people who have for generations been employed by one firm in one town are faced with the news that their plant may never open again. These are some of the downs of life.

There are two ways to handle these. One is to say, "Why me, Lord?" when the downers come, as they will. It is hard for me to understand the popularity of the book *When Bad Things Happen to Good People*. The title seems to indicate that if you're really good, trying hard, full of faith, then bad things ought not to happen to you. Where did we ever get that idea? Not from the Bible. Bad things happen to good people and bad people, to faith-filled people and faithless people. My friend Art Greer, writer and preacher, claims he knows why some people like church. "It's because it's the one place bad things can't happen to them for one hour in the week. The toilet doesn't get stopped up, the sink doesn't run over, the phone won't ring, and the school principal can't call to say, 'I've got your son or daughter here in the office.' No downers can happen in church. The only price you pay for that hour of bliss is the possibility of being bored by the preacher." The good and the bad, the ups and downs, happen to everybody. That's the way life is.

The second way to handle the ups and downs is to be aware that life proceeds like a sine wave. That's the line on a graph that looks like a continuous, undulating wave. The good news is that you and I have the power to draw the zero-point line through our sine wave. Everything below is bad and everything above is good. What is an upper and what is a downer on the sine wave of your life? You can decide. Depending on the zero point, you can have lots of uppers or endless downers.

The same friend I referred to just above, Art Greer, has written a book entitled *There Are No Grownups in Heaven.* In it he says that his theology (and I confess at first this idea blew me away) is that some people always find a parking place while some people never find one. Now think about that. Is he saying there is some magic for the believer who goes downtown, convinced a place will open? I don't think so. I think it works like this. One person may say, "I went downtown today, I prayed and God found me a parking place only two blocks away. What a miracle!" The next person says, "Rats! I prayed for a parking spot and three people got closer to the front door than I did." What constitutes a miracle for you? How close must your parking spot be before you rate it an upper or a downer?

I have a number of friends who worship regularly at the Crystal Cathedral where Bob Schuller is founding pastor. They tell me that at least one big attraction (besides the preacher) is that there's plenty of parking space. It's true they have plenty of parking, but think for a minute. At the Crystal Cathedral you may actually park your car four blocks away, but you're still on their campus. It's all in your mind. At our church, if you park two blocks away, you say, "Darn! The church parking lot was filled and we had to walk two blocks." I have suggested we draw a big imaginary square around our church and consider that area our campus. Then we all get to park right on campus. Again, where do you set your zero line? Life is often what you expect, which, incidentally, is why for the pessimist, every pleasant occurrence is a surprise.

Think of the possible report Paul could have given when he returned to Antioch after his first missionary journey. He could have said, "Do you know what you guys got us into? To begin with, we sailed on an old, leaky ship with a stinking bilge and I was seasick the whole time. When we got to where we were going, we were persecuted and stoned and the opposition was fierce. Am I glad to be home!" Instead, I'm sure he said something like this:

"Listen, let me tell you about the mighty acts of God. We got there and the response in Iconium and Derbe and Lystra was phenomenal. Now God has churches all over that area—faithful people who are our brothers and sisters in Christ. Oh, yes, we had persecution, but God delivered us." How do we report on our personal history? Do we cheer or complain? I suggest that depends on where we have set the zero point on our sine wave.

Finally, let me suggest that since we're going to have downers, and the Bible promises we will have them, in spite of our faith, we try to make them quality downers. Let's get the most mileage we can out of them. That's part of the secret of grace. I don't suggest we seek downers—that is sick. We have sometimes heard in the church that suffering is good for its own sake, it makes you identify with God. The more you suffer, the more God-like you'll be. I want to say loud and clear that Jesus suffered once and for all for everyone, and His job is taken. We should never seek suffering, but we *will* suffer and we *will* have downers of all kinds and we have to learn to make the most of them.

Here Paul reports on the positive aspects of his journey to the church at Antioch. But listen to what he says in 2 Corinthians 11:24–27: "Five times I have received at the hands of the Jews the forty lashes less one. Three times I have been beaten with rods; once I was stoned. Three times I have been shipwrecked; a night and a day I have been adrift at sea; on frequent journeys, in danger from rivers, danger from robbers, danger from my own people, danger from Gentiles, danger in the city, danger in the wilderness, danger at sea, danger from false brethren; in toil and hardship, through many a sleepless night, in hunger and thirst, often without food, in cold and exposure." And then he adds, almost in an aside, "Apart from other things, there is the daily pressure upon me of my anxiety for all the churches." Paul is saying, "I'll give you credentials. Look at me. I have really suffered." And that suffering gives credibility to his witness.

Joe Bayly, author of many books and vice president of David C. Cook Publishing Company, lost his young daughter, and out of the pain of that experience he wrote a book that has blessed many.

That must be one of the ultimate downers, the loss of a child, and yet many have been blessed by their story. Oddly enough, people want to hear about your downers. When you tell them only about your uppers, you are a bore. How you managed and how you survived when that awful catastrophe struck is interesting. If you are at a party and you want to bore those gathered around you, say, "I want to tell you about my cross-country trip. We drove seven thousand miles and never had any mishaps. We started out from Seattle and went first to Spokane—" Believe me, people will drift away one by one or in great droves. A pastor on our staff, Ray Moore, took his wife and family on a seven-thousand-mile cross-country trip last summer. They came back with the wildest tales of all that went wrong—all the storms, the wrong turns, the flat tires—and the congregation loved it.

Some people can't even enjoy their uppers. They agonize about a job change, and after much prayer, they get just the offer they want. Immediately, they begin to worry that they may fail or that the company might go under. The very first day on the job they are full of anxiety about the future. I hope you can enjoy your uppers, but beyond that, we Christians ought to be able to enjoy even the downers. We can say, "Well, this hurts now. But some day I'm going to find a use for this experience."

Every creature has a protective device, one which is fairly obvious. A turtle has a shell, the skunk gives a smell, the eagle has claws and a beak, the elephant has great size. What do we humans have? We have discernment—discernment about what's happening to us and around us. We can see God in the ups and celebrate, and we can see Him in the downs, when it hurts. We can say, "God, I want to use this for you. I'm glad you are here with me." We can all affirm the truth of Romans 8:28: "All things work together for good to them that love God, to them who are the called according to His purpose" (KJV).

Wind & Fire

CHAPTER FIFTEEN

Snapshots from the Family Album

ACTS 16, 17, 18

I can recall feeling really embarrassed as a teenager when I brought home a guest and my parents hauled out the family album and displayed all those pictures of me from babyhood on. I thought I would never do anything so gauche to my children—but I did. Our only daughter was married last year, and at Christmas she and her new husband came out to celebrate with us in Seattle. Naturally, he was eager to know more about this girl he'd married. I was glad to oblige. Much to her chagrin, we got out the family album.

Our very first picture of Christine shows her at six months old, naked as a jaybird, lying on a rug. In later snapshots she is graduating from a Lutheran kindergarten in Illinois wearing a cap and gown. Then there were the high school pictures, many snapped with her best boyfriend, Huey. I always kind of liked Huey, a fine, hard-working fellow who was planning to be a dentist. One of the college photos has Chris riding on a motorcycle behind some guy I was a whole lot less enthusiastic about. I remember feeling greatly relieved when that romance broke up. In some of the last pictures she is working behind her desk in a Florida Rural Legal Services office. The album seems to take in the whole sweep of our daughter's life to date, and yet it in no way tells Matthew who this person is he has married. If and when you marry, you marry a mystery. Thirty years later you are still married to a mystery; at least that's my experience.

In that same sense, God is a mystery. God is not a principle, a philosophy, a doctrine. You can't know Him as you would chemistry and algebra and history. He's a person, and when you meet and give your life to that Person, He is still a mystery, no matter how long that relationship continues. Nevertheless, we can endeavor to learn something about this mystery, divine or human, in one of two ways. The first is to study the subject through a microscope, burrowing in and trying to get an in-depth perspective as a psychoanalyst does through years of analysis. Another way is the kind of sweep through the family album that we have just described.

All through this study of Acts, we've been attempting to learn more about the Holy Spirit. And in these next chapters, we'll try to do that by examining some snapshots of the Holy Spirit in the family album—the Bible. That's where we find graphic word pictures of all our spiritual ancestors—Abraham, Moses, David, Peter, James, Mary, Lydia, Priscilla and Aquila. Captured as they are in our unique family album, we can go back and examine those pictures and learn about our heritage. For our purposes, I'd like to assume that chapters 16, 17 and 18 of Acts are part of that family album, and see if we can find some well-defined snapshots of the Holy Spirit.

We'll depart from the usual study of these chapters in a second way. Most students of the Book of Acts study the people, the events, and, particularly, the activities of Paul. Let's for the moment compare Paul to a surfer. We see him, figuratively, taking all kinds of wild waves. He bobs up and down, tumbling, falling, riding the crest. Now, rather than focusing on Paul, we're going to focus on the wave. Remember, the surfer doesn't make the wave. He or she simply rides it, well or poorly. The wave that carries us along, as the church of Jesus Christ, is the Holy Spirit. Our job is to ride that wave the best we know how.

With that preamble, look with me at the seven snapshots I've gathered of the Holy Spirit in these next chapters. The first is found in chapter 16, beginning at verse 6. Paul and Silas are beginning the third missionary journey. They attempt to go into Bithynia, but, we are told, "the Spirit of Jesus did not allow them," and so they went instead down to Troas. Here, through a vision, Paul is told to "come over to Macedonia and help us." Let's call this photo "The Macedonian Vision," with a subtitle, "Who's in Charge?"

We learn two things in this little glimpse of the Holy Spirit. One concerns the identity of the Spirit. Luke, the writer of Acts, and Paul, call Him the Spirit of Jesus. We worship one God, not three. We know Him as the Creator-Father, as our Savior and Lord Jesus, and as the Holy Spirit. The Holy Spirit is the Spirit of Jesus, and the creative Spirit of God the Father, but the Spirit is the *present tense of God.* Jesus left heaven, came to live among us, was killed, raised from the dead, and ascended into heaven. God is with us now in the person of the Holy Spirit.

The second lesson we learn from this one little snapshot is that the Spirit is able to intervene and direct the lives of believers. As we have noted, Paul wants to go to Bithynia but instead is given a vision which sends him to Macedonia. Thus, for the first time, the gospel is brought to Europe. The first European convert is a woman, a rich merchant, Lydia, a seller of purple goods. She is the prepared person who receives the good news gladly, and through her Christianity is launched in Europe.

The Spirit can operate in our lives just as He did in Paul's. There are times when He seems to say "no," and our path is blocked. Another time, a door opens unexpectedly, and we can go through it. He can direct us in terms of when to start that business or make that call.

I meet Tuesday mornings with a group of men to pray and read

the Bible. One of the men was concerned for his business partner,
a man in his late forties who was dying. My friend said, "We never
talked about the really important things, about life and death. Pray
that I may have a chance to do that this week. He has only a short
time to live and I want him to know about the Lord and His love."
He made the call that week, but somehow the opportunity was not
there. There were other visitors and many interruptions. The next
week he reported to us, "I tried, but I failed. I think the Spirit said
'no.'" Just days later, the dying man called my friend to come
over. They spent three uninterrupted hours and opened their
hearts to each other.

Snapshot #1, then, reveals who is in charge of the church. No
hierarchy, no group of officers, no long-range planning committee decided that it was the right time to bring the Gospel to Europe.
The Spirit chose the time, and the church responded in obedience
to that Spirit.

The second snapshot is found in verses 16 through 18. Paul and
Silas, while going to the place of prayer, are met by a slave girl with
a spirit of divination. Her soothsaying has produced much profit
for her owners. For many days she has followed Paul and Silas
about, crying, "These men are servants of the most high God, who
proclaim to you the way of salvation." In annoyance, Paul turns
and charges the spirit to come out of her, and she is healed. I
would give snapshot #2 the title "The Slave Girl Healed," and the
subtitle "The Holy Spirit Is Comfortable with Imperfect People."
The snapshot captures the truth that the treasure of the Holy Spirit
is in earthen vessels, namely, us, and I love its earthy, nonspiritual
flavor. In fact, if the story had been mine to tell, I probably would
have told it so differently.

My version probably would go like this: Paul is preaching the
riches of Christ and suddenly he is moved by compassion for this
girl who has been crying out in agony for several days. Filled with
pity and the Spirit of Jesus, he turns to help her, he lays hands on
her, prays for her and she is healed, and he sends her off with his
blessings. It didn't happen that way, according to Luke. This
fanatic little evangelist has a laser-beam vision, pinpointed on

preaching the Gospel in season and out of season, and all the while she's calling out in her disturbed state, "Oh, listen to this man, listen to this man." Finally Paul has had enough. She has busted up his meeting once too often. In annoyance, he says something like, "For heaven's sake, in Jesus' name, be healed and get out of here!"

Another reason I love that story is that it puts the whole issue of motivation in proper perspective. In every endeavor, the Spirit does the work. He lives in us and speaks through us; we have only to be there. We may sometimes welcome an interruption on a busy day. It might be a dear friend, and we sit and have coffee and share and pray together. The Spirit can use that encounter. But, if you're like me, you're sometimes annoyed by interruptions, even feeling resentful about this person who is ruining our schedule. We don't have an hour to give them, and we feel pressured. But even though we may not feel good about this interruption, who cares? The Spirit has put us in that situation and if we can keep our mind and heart open, He'll do the rest. The Holy Spirit can act whether our motives are high or low, loving or otherwise.

The third snapshot of the Holy Spirit, which we'll call "Songs in the Night," is found in verses 25 to 34 of chapter 16. The men who lost their livelihood when the slave girl was healed managed to have Paul and Silas thrown in prison. It must have been one similar to those old New England prisons, for their feet were fastened in stocks. At midnight, Paul and Silas were praying and singing hymns when a great earthquake shook the foundations of the prison and all the doors were opened and all the fetters unfastened. When the jailer awoke and saw what had happened he drew his sword, about to kill himself. In those times, if prisoners escaped, the jailer received their sentence. He was just about to save the authorities the trouble of executing him when Paul called out and reassured him that the prisoners were all there. The jailer rushed in, fell down before Paul and Silas, then brought them out and said, "Men, what must I do to be saved?" They spoke the word of the Lord to him and to the members of his household, and that very night he was baptized with all his family.

When you really believe that God, the ultimate being, loves
you, you're home free. That's why in snapshot #3 we find Paul
and Silas singing songs in the night. Paul and Silas didn't know
that they would be delivered. They might have been killed. But
there they are, locked in the stocks, singing hymns, praising God
and holding a revival meeting in prison. This is not because they
expect deliverance but because they are riding the rising tide of the
Spirit. Their immediate fate is unimportant, for they are connected now and for all time to that great force moving through
history and the cosmos. Billy Graham was once asked how he
could be so optimistic. He said, "I've read the last chapter of the
book." That's the certainty we need to sing songs in the night.
There are no guarantees about the future, but ultimately we can
say, as Paul did in his letter to Timothy, "For I know whom I have
believed, and I am sure that he is able to guard until that Day what
has been entrusted to me" (2 Tim. 1:12). That's the Paul who was
able to sing songs in the night with Silas.

If you are subject to sleepless nights, wakeful and beset by anx-
ieties and pressures, I hope you can begin to sing songs and to say,
"Lord, I face a tough day tomorrow, but my life is yours and I'm
trusting you." That kind of supreme confidence is the mark of the
Spirit. When you and I are in tight places we can believe that He
who is in us is greater than he who is in the world.

Snapshot #4 is taken in Thessalonica. Paul has been preaching
there for three weeks and making converts among the Greeks and
many of the leading women. Again, the Jews are perturbed. They
gather the crowd and set the city in an uproar. The charge is that
"these men who have turned the world upside down have come
here also." My title for this snapshot is "The Holy Spirit's Trouble-
makers." The subtitle might be "Blandness Is a Heresy." If we
belong to the Holy Spirit, we cannot settle for the status quo, or for
"business as usual." We are those committed to a more excellent
way. We are challenging the power structures and principalities of
our time. That's a mark of the Holy Spirit.

The American Revolution has sometimes been called the Presbyterian Revolution because so many Presbyterian clergy were

instrumental in that revolution. The Holy Spirit's people are in the forefront of positive change. The true church is historically a revolutionary church, a trouble-making church.

Let's move on to snapshot #5. Paul has been preaching in the boondocks, the minor leagues, and getting a great response. When there is once again opposition in Beroea, a neighboring town of Thessalonica, Paul is sent off to Athens, leaving Silas and Timothy behind. He arrives in the university center of the world. Athens' great days of glory were past, but the city was still the great hub of learning, the Oxford or Cambridge of its time. In that marvelous, rarefied atmosphere, Paul goes to Mars Hill, where the scholars and philosophers gather each day to hear something new. This worldly bunch has heard it all. They sit all day just exchanging ideas, not too unlike our present academic scene—much talk and theorizing and very little action. We all get caught up in that sometimes. My wife says I'm a newsaholic. I love to sit in front of the TV in the evening and hear the world's gossip, even though it's much the same every day. There are the inevitable earthquakes and floods, politics and wars, but I'm addicted to hearing about it all and I understand those Athenians.

Paul's audience is made up of these people who want to sit around and discuss great ideas. He gets their attention by building a bridge, by commenting on their many statues to their gods. He moves on to talk about the one true God, but when he mentions Jesus being raised from the dead, he loses them. Some mock him and, even worse, others say, in effect, "Tell us about this later." The title of this snapshot is "Flop in Athens." Paul has his big moment and he blows it. The suggested subtitle for this one is "The Holy Spirit Keeps Us Humble." A small company did believe and joined Paul, but for the most part, the crowd said, "Ho hum. We'll come back and hear you another time." But the real mark of spiritual maturity, for the Apostle Paul, or for you and me, is how we deal with failure. How do we handle it when we blow the big one? We hoped so much to accomplish some particular goal, and as far as we can tell, we flopped. Paul seems able to say, "Well, win some, lose some," and moves on. Too often, in that situation, most of us spend endless time wallowing around, paralyzed by our failure. Paul never missed a beat. He just kept on preaching.

Snapshot #6 is found at the beginning of chapter 18. Paul moves on from Athens to Corinth. He is befriended there by Priscilla and Aquila, who are also tentmakers. He moves in with them and they begin to ply their trade together. We'll call this photo "The Rhythm of Life." Paul sits eight or ten hours a day sewing tents, and by night he continues to be the world's most exciting evangelist and preacher. I think the Holy Spirit wants that same rhythm of life for all of us. It's a strange thing for a preacher to say, but I confess I'm a little suspicious of the religious professionals. It's a somewhat lopsided focus. It seems to me it's much healthier to have a job out there in the real world. We need the rhythm of life—prayer and play, work and worship. All the while Paul is in Corinth, about a year and a half, he is the center of violent controversy—preaching, converting, challenging his opponents. And yet we have a picture of this "eye of the hurricane figure" sitting quietly, sewing all day with his colleagues. It's a wonderful reminder of the rhythm of life.

The last photo, snapshot #7, is entitled "The Lay Ministry," and we find it in Acts 18:24. Apollos, an eloquent preacher, versed in Scripture, arrives in Ephesus. He begins to speak and teach about Jesus, though he knows only the baptism of John. When Priscilla and Aquila hear him, they take him aside and explain to him the gospel of Jesus more accurately. He moves on to Achaia, where he greatly helps new Christians there and publicly confronts the Jews through Scripture to prove that Jesus is the Christ. You could subtitle the lay ministry photo "The Holy Spirit's Strategy." Two laymen, Priscilla and Aquila, hear this powerful pulpiteer and have the discernment to realize he doesn't have the total message. His message is like John's, that of repentance—shape up and change your ways. He is unaware that Christ, through the Holy Spirit, is here and that He can dwell in us and change our lives. Even preachers today aren't above correction from laymen filled with the Holy Spirit.

Snapshot #7 is one that gives us great hope that the Spirit is indeed in charge of the church. But all the other snapshots we have just looked at are part of a much bigger album, the one which captures that wave, that riptide through history which continues throughout the world. And you and I are called to be those who are repeatedly catching and riding that tidal wave. My colleague Ray Moore took a couple of friends out on a twelve-foot boat on Puget Sound last summer. At one point, they found themselves in the path of an enormous tanker. The passengers were scared silly, but not Ray. With that twelve-foot boat and a small outboard motor, he headed right for the tanker and began surfing in its huge wake. There's a lesson for us all—to get in our twelve-foot boat, to find the wave of the Spirit going through our lives, and to get on top of it and go.

CHAPTER SIXTEEN

The Church and the Culture Crunch

ACTS 19, 20

There have been any number of divisive issues in the
church over the years. Today one of our most serious
divisions arises over the church's view of and role in our present
culture. Think of the people and groups whose names automati-
cally raise strong reactions in us—pro and con. There are the
Berrigan brothers, who sprinkled blood on government docu-
ments to protest our nation's Vietnam policies. Some churchmen
cheered and some booed. The recent rise of the Moral Majority
has delighted some and horrified others. But these Christians are
endeavoring to affect the culture of today and redefine the
church's role in that culture. I live in Seattle, Washington, and
our best-known citizen, familiar throughout the world to our nation's enemies and allies alike, is Bishop Hunthausen. His protest
of nuclear proliferation is an attempt to affect our nation's policy
and, in the larger sense, our culture.

The world's best-known evangelist, Billy Graham, has, for most of his ministry, eschewed any interest in the social and political scene. He is reevaluating that position now and says, "Because I am a New Testament evangelist, I *must speak out* about the social scene." Right now, there is a great furor in Roman Catholic circles over Pope John Paul's visits to Third World or Iron Curtain countries. The pope pronounces vehemently and often that the clergy in those areas should not be involved in politics, and yet many defy him and consider such activities central to their Christianity.

It seems to me we can find out something of the role of the church in culture as we examine God's word to us in chapters 19 and 20 of Acts. We have there a picture of New Testament church life and we can see how it affects or collides with the culture of the first century. Chapter 19 begins with controversy on a theological issue. Paul meets a group of believers and asks if they have received the Holy Spirit since they believed. They have never heard of the Holy Spirit. Paul explains to them, as Priscilla and Aquila did for Apollos, that there are two baptisms, the baptism of John and the baptism of Jesus. They knew only about the baptism of John, which was far from good news. John's message was, "God knows who you are and He knows what you are doing. Shape up." That's bad news. The Good News is that God knows who you are and what you are doing *and* He is on your side.

John's baptism produced the religion of *oughts*. We ought to be better stewards, we ought to do more. Jesus' baptism changes those oughts to wants. We are so filled with God's love that we *want* to be more, to give more, to do more. One is a threat—shape up or ship out. The other is a gift—the gift of God's indwelling Spirit. One baptism emphasizes will power (e.g., I'm going to resolve from this day on to be more honest, more generous). In Jesus' baptism, we are hooked up with the river of living water, one that will never be exhausted. No more good resolutions are necessary. Instead, we tap into the main supply of God's own grace and power—the wind and fire of His Holy Spirit.

How did Paul perceive so quickly that these new Christians had not received the Holy Spirit's baptism? The Bible says, "Judge not," but that does not mean we can't be fruit inspectors. We can look for the fruit of the Spirit—love, joy, peace, patience, kindness, goodness, faithfulness, gentleness, self-control (Gal. 5:22). Those qualities are readily discernible. If you come into a worshiping community and the faces around you are gloomy and dourlooking, Paul's question is a valid one: "Have you received the Holy Spirit since you believed?"

Paul spends the next three months preaching to the Jews, and when they still disbelieve, he moves to a public hall. He moves out of the tight Jewish community and goes public. The result is that all of Asia hears the word of the Lord. God uses everything. Here he uses the rejection from one group to get the word out to a much bigger audience. We find Paul's ministry expanding, and extraordinary healings and miracles become commonplace. There is not enough of Paul to go around, and his personal clothing—handkerchiefs, aprons, and whatever—is carried away and laid on the sick, and they are healed. Even this phenomenon can be explained medically today. To live in the Spirit in a climate of hope, love, openness, confession, and joy is measurably therapeutic. No wonder miracles happened.

At this point, another perennial problem arises. Some very shrewd people see Paul's amazing power to heal the deepest physical and emotional needs, and they decide to copy him. The trouble is they begin to practice secondhand religion. They want to learn a bag of tricks. They don't want to *be* a Paul, but they want to do what he does. It's like praying to the God of our fathers. Unless we are also praying, "My God," the God of our fathers will not help us much. The God of our fathers has to become our personal God.

Unfortunately, most of us want to learn to *do* something, rather than to *be* something. Ministerial candidates go to seminary to learn how to help people. They'll learn many useful things in seminary, but they won't learn that. Only as the Holy Spirit dwells in us do we have the resources to help others. If we are hooked up to the river of living water, we transmit new life and new hope whenever we come on the scene. If you are tempted to learn techniques and methods and bypass becoming, remember the lesson here in the seven sons of Sceva. The evil spirit leapt out of the man they hoped to cure and beat them all up.

One of the most poignant memories of my seminary years concerns the night when some zealous students decided to evangelize that godless place next door called Princeton University. They gathered up thousands of empty pill capsules and stuffed them with Bible verses. They went through every dormitory, throwing these gospel bombs into each room, thinking somehow to reach the university for Jesus. Well, the university president called up our seminary president in short order with a strong protest. The next morning in chapel, our president and great missionary saint, John Mackay, was close to tears as he rebuked the culprits, saying something like this: "I don't question your zeal, but you have set back the cause of Christ in this place. It is my sincere desire that our seminary might be an influence on this great university. If you want to reach those students, go over there and make friends with them. Don't dash in and out with a bunch of tricks." So it is for all of us as Christians. We don't communicate the gospel with a string of clever techniques. We go out among others in vulnerable love and the power of the Holy Spirit.

In the next paragraph, we move onto the confrontation which most concerns us, that between Paul and the new believers and the culture. The silversmiths, who have been making shrines to Artemis, are getting worried. As a result of Paul's efforts, they are selling fewer and fewer statues. Artemis is the Greek name for the goddess Diana, and if you ever go to Ephesus, you can still buy a replica of her. She is a fertility goddess and her body is covered with breasts. She is too ridiculous to be obscene. You can still visit the huge amphitheater where the riot described in this Scripture took place. It's in disrepair, but still standing. The silversmiths felt their livelihood was being jeopardized and they stirred up the entire city against Paul. In their minds, they were simply protecting their way of life.

After hours of demonstrating, the crowd dispersed only when they learned they would be charged, by the Romans, with rioting. All through the tumult Paul was determined to go into the theater and face the mob, but his friends dissuaded him. His motto, even in the middle of a riot, was "safety last." When the uproar ceased, Paul departed again for Macedonia and spent the next months traveling throughout the region visiting the new Christians.

On the night before he was to set sail from Troas, Paul, the great evangelist, put part of his audience to sleep. He started a sermon at midnight and on this occasion he went on so long that a lad sitting in the window dozed off and fell two stories to what looked like his death. Paul went down immediately and restored him and then turned again to converse with his Christian friends for the rest of the night. It's comforting to know that on at least one occasion Paul was guilty of dull preaching. I heard about a stranger who wandered into the Sunday evening services in a little church in a tiny southern town. The preacher was going on and on and on. Turning to a man in the row behind him, the stranger asked, "How long has this man been preaching?" "Oh, about ten years," was the answer. "Well, in that case, I guess I'll stay. He must be about done by now." There is, of course, no end to the jokes about long, dull sermons. There is the poem that says,

> I never see my pastor's eyes,
> He hides their light divine.
> For when he prays, he closes his,
> And when he preaches, mine.

Well, that's what happened to the young lad named Eutychus.

In a larger sense, we must evaluate this scene of church life in Troas in light of the events in Ephesus. The church has suffered a serious clash with the culture, a clash of values. The Ephesian tradesmen have tried to put a stop to the spreading of the gospel, but nothing has changed. Paul continues preaching up and down the land, and new believers are added daily. When the power of the gospel touches pocketbooks, which is often where culture is most vulnerable, opposition is always at its fiercest. When Jesus cured a lunatic on the shores of Gadara, he encountered a strange reaction. The demoniac who had been running around cutting himself, spent some time with Jesus and was healed. I'm sure the townspeople who came out to find their neighbor well and whole and in his right mind, were impressed, but their question was, "Where are the pigs?" A whole herd of pigs was destroyed in the process of the healing, and for them the price was too high. "We prefer the pigs," they seemed to say. "Would you please leave?"

Hundreds of thousands of people in our nation are engaged in the defense industry. Some of them are members of our church in Seattle. What happens if the church takes a firm stand on unilateral disarmament and we are able to effect a reduction in our nation's arms buildup? It will mean the loss of jobs for these Christian brothers and sisters, and they will, understandably, not be happy about that. That's presently an important issue in terms of the church and the culture crunch. I had lunch recently with a church member and he made a surprising statement. "I happen to believe in the new economic policies of our nation. I voted for our president, and I believe in what he is doing. I'm about to go bankrupt, but I really feel that if I have to go bankrupt in order for our country to get back on a sound fiscal policy, it's OK." His own life and livelihood are expendable because of his principles. That's a kind of spiritual heroism.

As we consider the church and the culture crunch, it seems to me that at least two errors are possible. One is to insist that the church's only business is to save souls. That's what happened to the church in Nazi Germany. Most church leaders just kept quiet, served communion, and preached sermons. Few would condone their course of action. On the other hand, we can believe that the only purpose of the church is to change culture. That's also heretical. The Christian message is more than social reform. We have a classic illustration in George Bernard Shaw's *Major Barbara*, where the contrast is drawn between the Salvation Army and its work and the empire of England's leading industrialist, a munitions manufacturer. We find him saying, "My company provides jobs, security and welfare for my workers. What more can the church do for people?" Certainly, the church's job is much larger than that. Our objective is building the Kingdom of God.

The Gospel is both personal and social. At its best, the church throughout history has been both. In the past, Christians have been almost solely responsible for the abolition of slavery in most parts of the world. The church has been responsible for child welfare and a society where children have rights and are not simply treated as property. The church is in the forefront of the establishment of public schools, hospitals, orphanages. The church, at its best, has been the leaven and the light that has changed the way the world lives. The church, aside from talking about a King and a Kingdom, must confront the culture of its time and affect that culture in terms of the rights of all people.

As we said, we abhor the stance of the church in Nazi Germany, which seemed to say, in effect, "Let Hitler do what he wants. We're here to sing hymns and save souls." On the other hand, I would not want to belong to a church that advocates a theocracy, something like Calvin's Geneva, where a group of zealous believers, elders and pastors, ran a city. I'm too strong a believer in individual liberty for that. We need to find some middle course between being uninvolved and wanting to run the nation our way. Incidentally, in a new book called *Trading with the Enemy*, Charles Higham claims he accidentally discovered because of the Freedom of Information Act, irrefutable proof that Hitler could not have begun World War II or waged that war without the help of many of our major businesses in America, and with the consent of the American government. In other words, willing ignorance was not just the problem of the church in Germany. What role could or should the church in America have played during that conspiracy of silence?

What do we do today as Jesus' people, followers of The Way, confronted by a nuclear situation in which fifty thousand warheads are available for use by the two superpowers? That translates into the equvalent of three and a half tons of TNT for every man, woman, and child in the world. I don't have any simple solutions. I am a former World War II combat infantry sergeant and far from a pacifist, but I say something must be done, and you and I as the church must stand for some positive alternatives. Our nation proposes to spend one and a half trillion dollars in the next five years for defense. Someone explained that to me. "If you began on the day of Jesus' birth to spend a million dollars a day, you would not by now, have spent even half of it." That's how much money we're going to spend in the next five years to save ourselves from the unknown horror.

There are so many other complicated issues that you and I as Christians must address, and not necessarily corporately. Women's issues, abortion, central or decentralized government, obligations to the Third World, the present welfare system. I have brothers and sisters in Christ whom I honor who are on both sides of many of these questions. I'm not advocating that the church move in lockstep, but, if we, as God's people, don't care about the culture crunch, we are less than God's people.

In Romans 12:2, Paul says, "Don't be conformed to this world. Be transformed by the renewal of your mind." Years ago, as I was riding in a New York cab, the driver and I were talking about the coming mayoral election. I asked, "How are you going to vote?" He said, "Well, my grandfather and my father and I have always voted the party line. But there comes a time in life when you have to put aside your principles and do the right thing."

Sometimes even we Christians have to put aside our principles and do the right thing. Listen to what Dr. Martin Luther King, Jr., said: "In no sense do I advocate evading or defying the law. That would lead to anarchy. An individual who breaks a law that conscience tells him is unjust or who willingly accepts the penalty of imprisonment in order to arouse the conscience of the community over its injustice is in reality expressing the highest respect for the law." We don't break the law without paying a price. On the other hand, new laws are not enough to make us a godly, righteous nation. Jesse Jackson has traveled up and down the land speaking to the poorest of the blacks in some of our terrible ghettos. He says, "In the final analysis, freedom will ultimately come from your house and my house and not from the White House." He is saying that the principles of freedom must begin on a personal level.

A recent Gallup Poll has predicted that a profound religious revival will occur in the final two decades of the twentieth century. There are indications that that prediction is correct. But what kind of a revival will it be? If it is *only* a personal one, or *only* a social one, we are in trouble. I profoundly hope that God will call His people to discover the deeply personal dimensions of a relationship with Him and to one another. And that has implications for the future wherever Christian people live. In Deuteronomy 4:25–31, God warns His people to beware of idols made with hands. Idols made with hands will never save them. But if His people turn from those idols and seek the living God, there is hope and blessing for them and for the world.

We worship any number of idols made with hands today—not just the weapons in our nuclear arsenal, but our economy, our political systems, our unions, our institutions, and "my job." When these are in conflict with what the Spirit of God tells us about truth and justice, we must speak out for change. The Lord alone is our authority and guide, and the church in the New Testament tradition makes all culture subject to Him.

Wind & Fire

CHAPTER SEVENTEEN

Saved from Religion

ACTS 21, 22, 23

About a year ago Dolphus Weary, a tall and engaging black man, was in town to meet with some of our church groups. He is director of a Christian lifestyle center in Mendenhall, Mississippi, where our church sends interns each summer. In talking with our staff, someone asked him how God got hold of him. He was glad to tell us. He said, "I grew up in a very religious part of the country, and in a very church-centered small town, as most towns in the deep South are. My family was religious and went to church regularly—one where testimonies were given from time to time about being saved from alcoholism, or drug addiction, resentments or depressions, things like that. I was slated to be hopelessly religious the rest of my life. When I had my Damascus Road experience, I realized that I had been saved from religion."

I was reminded of Dolphus and his story once again as I read these next chapters of Acts. It seems to me the whole drama of the

Book of Acts reflects the conflict between religion and the new life
God wants to give us. The conflict comes to a climax in these three
chapters. All that has gone before has been the prelude for this
great culmination. The major theme throughout the symphony,
as we said, has been the mighty work of the Holy Spirit rather than
the acts of the Apostles. The Holy Spirit has been acting through
faithful followers of the Way such as Paul, Silas, Barnabas, Timothy, Cornelius, Lydia, Priscilla and Aquila. To use our image
once more, they saw the Spirit rising like a tidal wave throughout
the world and they got out their surfboards and began to ride out
that wave. Acts is the story of those who are swept along, captured
by the Spirit. Sometimes there is a horrendous wipe-out—persecution, imprisonment, stonings. But they get back on their
boards to catch the wave once again.

The main theme of this symphony in Acts, then, is the Holy
Spirit blowing new life into the world, from Jerusalem and Antioch to Asia Minor and Europe and finally to Rome and the whole
civilized world. But the subtheme of the opus is opposition, criticism, persecution, and hatred. And we discover, especially in
these next chapters of Acts, that the opposition comes most of all
from the religious. We see the collision, not so much between the
gospel and the world, as between the gospel and religion. Actually,
we're all religious. The word comes from the Latin *religio*, meaning "to bind," and we are all bound by our particular interpretation of life, whether we are communists, reactionaries, atheists, or
hedonists. The whole biblical message in its essence is that God
has come in Jesus Christ to set us free from that bondage.

Let me confess here that I am addicted to horror films. My
daughter and I have always loved them, and she and I will sit up
until two or three in the morning to watch these old grade-B
movies. My favorites are the Dracula movies. Fortunately for me,
they keep being remade. You know the plot. Some unknown
horror is stalking the townspeople. Victims are turning up with
these little puncture marks on their necks. The citizens band
together to fight this threat and save themselves and their families.
Finally, at the conclusion of the film, somebody figures out where

this evil, life-destroying force is coming from. It's coming from some presence in that old castle. The last scene is my favorite. The townspeople go off to do battle with the evil itself, armed with stakes and mallets, with crucifixes and holy water.

I'd like to think there's some moral in these horror films. If you are being plagued by some adversary, the best strategy is to go on the offensive against the enemy. That's precisely what Paul does here. His mission is to proceed ultimately to Rome, the center of power and authority, and to proclaim the Gospel to the world from that central point. Before doing that, he wants to return one more time to the source of all the opposition and offer them one more chance to change. He interrupts his journey to Rome to go back to Jerusalem. It is one more walk into Dracula's castle, if you will, crucifix in hand.

In the beginning of the chapter we find one of the most touching incidents in the Book of Acts. All along the way Paul's journey is interrupted. He must stop to change boats, get his sandals repaired, or find fresh horses, and each time he meets with a handful of local believers—the church. As Paul travels through, they share their homes, their food, and their lives. They share tears and pray for him. William Barclay has said, "The man who is within the family of the church is better equipped with friends than any other man in all the world."

We Christians have astonishing connections. I doubt that there is a major city in the world where you could not find a handful of people with whom the Lord has made you one. In most cases, they would probably take you in and share whatever they have with you. That's the underground church, those clusters of people knit together by Jesus Himself. Those Christians who are sent by industry to far-flung places can claim that connection all over the world. They are sure to find members of the family to whom they belong. All along his route, Paul met with groups like that. In this case, fearing for his safety, they pled with him not to pursue his plans to go to Jerusalem, and we are given that poignant picture of the little company on the beach, men, women and children, kneeling together in prayer. Further along the route, the church at

Caesarea again entreated Paul with tears not to continue to Jerusalem, but he could not be dissuaded.

   In Jerusalem at last, Paul meets with the disciples and he is told
to try to placate these religious people, the high priests. They
suggest something dramatic—to take a vow, to shave his head, and
to purify himself along with four other men, whose expenses he
would underwrite. Paul agrees, but before the days of purification
are up, the Jews from Asia, his bitter opponents, see him in the
temple and stir up the crowd so that Paul is dragged out by the mob
and would have been beaten to death if not for the intervention of
Roman soldiers.

   Imagine, if you will, that you are a film director doing the story
of the life of Paul and shooting this scene. There is the legendary
cast of thousands, crowded on Solomon's Porch, the courtyard of
the temple, yelling, "Kill Paul! Kill Paul!" As this is about to
happen, a group of Roman soldiers who are there to keep the
peace, form a flying wedge and move into the crowd to rescue the
source of trouble, this wild little evangelist. They pick him up,
carry him over their heads on their shields, and hustle him
through the mob, who are all the while yelling, "Kill him! Kill
him!" Meanwhile, Paul is lying up there on the shield trying to
converse with the tribune in charge of this rescue operation. He
addresses him in good Greek, which makes a very positive impression. The tribune thought he was an Egyptian, a well-known
revolutionary. As they are carrying him up the stairs to the guard-
house, followed still by the angry crowd, Paul says, "Put me down.
I've got to talk to them." From the steps of the barracks, he begins
to give his personal witness. Our imaginary director would have a
hard time making this scene credible on film. Paul's holy boldness
can only be accredited to God's own Spirit in and with him.

   In chapter 20, a young man was literally bored to death by Paul's
sermon. But in this case, when Paul insists on speaking to the
lynch mob, they all fall silent. He had learned something from his
Mars Hill experience, and this time he attempts no such clever or
subtle sermon but gives them his witness: "A funny thing happened to me on the way to Damascus." But even before he gets

into the story of how he met Jesus, he speaks to the crux of their complaints. They think he is not religious enough. He trots out his credentials. He recites his background, his education, his status, his zeal to persecute Christians. Then he proceeds to say that he would have been just like them except for someone called Jesus who interrupted his life on the way to Damascus. The crowd reacts with outrage.

For the second time, the soldiers can barely save Paul from the mob and they haul him into the barracks. They decide to scourge him, but Paul pulls rank. He states that he is a Roman citizen, which dismays the tribune. On the next day, he calls together the chief priests and the rest of Paul's accusers in an attempt to discover what this man's crime is. This is a moment of high drama. Paul stands before the religious people, his implacable foes.

His first statement, "Brethren, I have lived before God in all good conscience up to this day," causes the high priest to have him struck on the mouth. To the religious that claim is blasphemy. Nobody has a good conscience. That is not an option. The number and variety of rules were such that no one could possibly keep them. Obviously, anyone with a good conscience has missed the whole point of Jewish legalism. Nothing is settled by this new hearing except that forty people make a vow to kill Paul and neither to eat nor to drink until the deed is done. Paul is warned by his nephew and enlists the help of the tribune. By night a huge Roman guard conducts him safely to Caesarea and to a hearing before Governor Felix.

We might wonder what happened to those forty men who were unable to keep their vow. Did they all drop dead of hunger and thirst? I rather doubt it. As we said, *religio*, the Latin root word of "religion," means to tie down or bind back. The religious take vows, carry out rituals, follow precise and intricate laws. We could compare it to the image of Gulliver, the giant washed ashore in the land of the tiny people. While he is still sleeping they put their ropes, which for Gulliver are actually threads, all around his arms and legs and body. When Gulliver awakes, he cannot move. He is tied down until they learn to trust him and cut him loose. That is the kind of binding done in the name of religion—millions of tiny restrictions which ultimately render us immobile. We say of somebody who behaves compulsively that he or she did it religiously. That is not meant as a compliment. It means that person is under some unexplainable drive to behave in a certain way.

The conflict here, in its essence, is the one between law and grace. God has entered the world in Jesus offering a whole new way of life and often those who want to settle for religion cannot handle such freedom. Religion masquerades as other things—certainty, safety, tradition, predictability. We're told that conservative churches have been growing in the past decade. Perhaps one reason is that they offer certainty and safety. They tell you what to believe and how to behave. We love those clear directives, because we don't want to live with ambiguity or uncertainty.

We might ask what place the Bible plays in making this choice between religion and freedom, between law and grace. Your Bible can be a rulebook that binds you into a way of life. You study it to be sure you are not missing any of the rules. Or, you can see your Bible as a love letter from God. Certainly it contains rules, but it reassures us that when we fail we are forgiven and that God has great plans for us.

I have a friend who, when he got converted some years ago, also got religious—at least at first. He was one of those people who demanded a proof text for everything. His wife had been urging him to help more around the house, but he had very clear ideas in those days of what were men's jobs and what were women's jobs. He finally said to her, "Unless you can show me a biblical text that says that I should be helping you in the kitchen, I don't plan to." That's all she needed. She prayed, read her King James Bible, and finally found one. She read to him from 2 Kings 21:13: "God says, 'I will wipe Jerusalem as a man wipeth a dish, wiping it, and turning it upside down.'" That's one way to use your Bible—to search for rules to cover every aspect of life.

There are all sorts of Christian groups these days who want to give us new sets of rules. They hold week-long seminars where you can fill your notebooks with instructions on how to behave as a

Christian family. One of the large international campus ministries published a book a few years ago purporting to instruct us in how Christians look. In it we are shown drawings of a variety of faces—the victorious face, the loving face, the faith-filled face—and readers are encouraged to practice making the faces of a Christian. What a travesty on the message of freedom that we find in the Bible. The true walk of faith must be filled with the unexpected. We come before God with awe and wonder, and we cannot learn some rote response to Him.

The Gospel is Good News. Jesus says, "If the Son makes you free, you will be free indeed" (John 8:36). We said earlier, all of us are by nature religious. We are comfortable when tied down to injunctions and rules. Christ comes along and snips those threads. We begin to move our arms and legs and to find that we can do things we never dreamed of. In Paul's encounter with the high priest, we find two different approaches to God. We can be guilty or grateful. The high priest was a master at producing guilt, as religious people usually are. But the Christian message is something far beyond that. Out of great gratitude, we love God and want to serve Him with all that we have and are.

Does such freedom lead to irresponsibility? Luther said, "Love God and sin boldly," but he was not promoting license. Rather, he meant finding what God's will is for our lives and living that out without fear of consequences. Paul's remark to the high priest did not mean his life was perfect, or that he never made a mistake, never was unloving or faithless. He was doing God's will. Sin is missing God's will for our life, and settling for religion perhaps is the ultimate sin because it can look so good, so like God's will. When we lie, cheat, and steal, we know we're sinning. But when we are religious, keeping all the rules, we may think we are doing God's will. Paul's accusers all look as if they are doing the right thing, and Paul challenges them and suggests there is a better way.

Earlier on, when all those Christian friends were remonstrating with Paul, urging him not to leave for Jerusalem, he said, "What are you doing, weeping and breaking my heart? For I am ready not only to be imprisoned but even to die at Jerusalem for the name of the Lord Jesus" (Acts 21:13). His attitude might have seemed to them irresponsible, but he was demonstrating that his life was expendable. He was giving it out of gratitude, not out of guilt. He had been set free from religion and he was free to lose his life in Jerusalem or wherever it might be required.

The gospel of freedom leads to a life of risk and uncertainty, and most of us are very uncomfortable with that. Religion, at its worst, produces arrogant, reactionary know-it-alls. They become God's patrons committed to defending Him, protecting His reputation. This attitude carried to extremes produced the Inquisition and the Salem witch hunts. This conflict between the religious and those who are free in Christ is inevitable. It's the difference between those who are experiencing God and those who are organizers of the experience of others. That's one of the pitfalls of theology or of church management. We organize the past experience into systems and programs. God continues to say, as He does in Isaiah 43:19, "Behold, I am doing a new thing." And each day we must respond to that new thing.

The gospel saves us from religion, but we are saved *for* something—to serve joyously and hilariously and to be expended in God's great causes. One such hilarious saint is a lady named Marie Emmanuelle, a Belgian nun who has taught for thirty-two years in the Grand College of Istanbul. Eleven years ago when the Vatican opened the doors to more vocational selectivity for women like Marie, she decided she had been teaching long enough. At age sixty-three, she petitioned to become a missionary, and she asked to serve in one of the poorest places in the world where the need was great. She went to Cairo, certainly one of the poorest cities in the world. The most desperately poor in Cairo are a group called the *Zabaline*, the city's 40,000 garbage collectors.

They spend their days gathering, with a little hand cart, a few bones, some rags, maybe a scrap of plastic or glass, and they live with their families on the city dumps without any of the amenities like sewers and water and electric light. Forty percent of their children die in their first year of life of tetanus and dysentery. This sixty-three-year-old nun lives there as well. She rises at 4:30 in the morning and picks her way across the dump, using a flashlight to scare off the wild dogs. She boards a bus, rides ten miles to attend mass, and then returns to her parish at the dump. She has built a kindergarten, a dispensary, a dental clinic, and a vocational school. She says of her experience, "These are the most beautiful years of my life." To me, Sister Marie Emmanuelle is someone who has been delivered from religion. Like Paul, she says out of gratitude, "Where can I serve? I'm expendable."

John Wesley, the father of the Methodist Church, said, "Do all the good you can by all the means you can in all the ways you can in all the places you can at all the times you can to all the people you can as long as ever you can." Not because you have to, but because you want to. You and I are saints. We are set free by Jesus Christ from any number of things including religion, and we are called to be saints in Cairo or Los Angeles or Chicago, or wherever He wants us. We are those set apart by God that He might do His extraordinary work through us.

CHAPTER EIGHTEEN

How to Witness

ACTS 24, 25, 26

In my second year of seminary, I was invited by a friend
to go to Calvary Episcopal Church in New York. Once a
month in their great hall a public meeting was held which attracted housewives, airline pilots, college students, and business-
men and women from all over the New York area. At each of those
meetings, four or five people would talk briefly about what God
was doing in their lives in the past days or weeks.

It was a whole new spiritual dimension for me. I grew up in a
great Gothic Presbyterian church with a glorious heritage, great
preaching, and gifted teachers. I was in seminary learning church
history, theology, and ethics and studying the Bible in the original
Greek and Hebrew. But I couldn't remember ever having heard
anyone say, "This week God did a marvelous thing in my life." It
was at that meeting to which my friend took me that my faith
moved from the historical and the academic into the dynamic
present, a much more frightening dimension for all of us. I realized I was called to preach—not just the good news of the past and

future, of a Jesus who lived once and would someday come again, but to witness to a present reality—the wind and fire of God's Spirit with us now.

Some months ago, a man came to see me who is not a member of our congregation. He said, "I am an agnostic, but I am worried about my son. He is a member of your church and he tells me he has a call from God to the ministry. What is that supposed to mean? What exactly is a call from God?" His son's experience made him question his own lack of faith for the first time. He could afford to be skeptical about events that were supposed to have happened some two thousand years ago. But he had never encountered a person, in this case his own son, who claimed that God had intervened in his life now. We spent a lively hour talking about God in the present tense, and then talking to Him in prayer.

That's what witnessing is all about—speaking about God in the present tense. In courtroom language, witnesses are not asked to interpret or editorialize or give opinions. They are to tell what they heard and saw: "I saw this person" . . . "I noticed this car" . . . "I heard a scream." Effective witnesses need no editorials. They are simply reporters of what they observed first hand, and that experience can't be dismissed easily.

Jesus says, "You shall receive power when the Holy Spirit has come upon you, and you shall be my witnesses . . ." (Acts 1:8). Only when this happens shall we be His witnesses. The Holy Spirit, as we have said, is the present tense of God. If we are believers, the Holy Spirit lives in us. If we were to add up all the power of God resident in a large church congregation, there would be no more than there is in one of us right now, because God cannot be divided. He is a person, not a force like electricity. The sum total of a congregation's capacity to contain God is no more than that of a single believer. If His Spirit dwells in us then life must be different wherever we go, and we simply bear witness to that difference.

The blind man whom Jesus healed was a powerful witness. The Pharisees tried to tell him that Jesus was a sinner and not able to perform such a sign. The man was adamant: "One thing I know.

Once I was blind and now I see." They kept asking him to repeat his story, but all he could tell them was what had happened to him. He was once blind and now he had his sight. That kind of witness may be monotonous, but it is powerful and irrefutable.

Claxton Monro, an Episcopal rector in Houston, Texas, wrote a book entitled *Witnessing Laymen Make Living Churches.* In it he says that the new reformation will occur in America and the Western world when the people of God learn the power of witness. I think there are indications in our cultural climate just now that the new era may be starting. We are being conditioned to give weight to personal testimonies. Most products being hawked on our TV sets are not endorsed by Ph.D.s or scientists or technical experts of various kinds. Some lady who looks like your next-door neighbor is recruited to sell you toilet paper. The guy trying to make you buy a certain brand of beer could be on your bowling team or a golfing buddy. The point is that these people are chosen because we can identify with them. They are folks just like us who are saying, "I tried it and it works." We are in a time like no other when Americans are prepared to hear and believe personal testimonies. The specialist is suspect. The woman next door is not. An army of God's people gossiping about their faith all across our land could be irresistible.

Most teaching and preaching are vehicles which call attention to all we have learned. But witnessing is a different dimension of communication. We are saying that the God who is changing our lives is available to the other person too. Witness was an important part of the communion service in the early church. Before the believers came to the Lord's table, someone would say, "Does anyone have any evidence for the hope that is in us?" One by one, these new Christians would stand up and give those reasons. "I had this resentment against my friend this week and after praying I went to her and asked for forgiveness." Or, "I had a physical problem and Jesus healed me." Or, "I was afraid and the Lord gave me courage." These communicants would witness to the fact that Jesus is alive. It's a custom that the church today might consider reinstating.

At Pentecost, everyone heard in his or her own language. That's still important in terms of witness. There is no one way to present Christ to your neighbor. While English is our common tongue, we Americans speak a number of sublanguages. There's the language of our social group. There's the language of our factory or office. There's the language of our profession or business. There's the language of our sorority or fraternity. There's the language peculiar to sailors or golfers or sports fans. Most of us have a good many of these languages at our disposal. We don't need to learn a new language, a religious language, or a spiritual language in order to communicate our faith. We can talk to our peers about Jesus in terms they will understand.

In chapter 26, we find Paul giving his witness, his last recorded speech in the Book of Acts. It is a climactic moment in the book. It's as if everything has been building to this confrontation between Paul and Agrippa and Festus. As we read it, we may recall that Jesus said to His disciples in Matthew 10:18–20: "You will be dragged before governors and kings for my sake, to bear testimony before them and the Gentiles. When they deliver you up, do not be anxious how you are to speak, what you are to say; for what you are to say will be given to you in that hour; for it is not you who speak, but the Spirit of your Father speaking through you." In this scene, Paul fulfills this prophecy of Jesus. He is dragged before the governor and king, and the Spirit speaks through him.

The scene is in a great meeting room, splendidly furnished, and hung with rich tapestries. The king, in all his finery and attended by his considerable retinue, is holding court. The governor is present. We can imagine the captains of the guard in their shining armor and the first citizens of the city, all richly garbed. The room is a riot of splendor and color. Into this awesome setting comes a small Jewish tentmaker in chains. Immediately he dominates the hall. The power of God is in him and he enters into dialogue with the king. Prior to this, Paul has spent two years languishing in prison under the governor, Felix. He may have used that time to sort through what he wants to say here. He has been waiting for two years for this hearing, and what does he say at this big moment in his life? He gives his witness!

Paul provides a wonderful example here of how to witness. First of all, he says he is fortunate to be there. He is glad to have a chance to tell Agrippa what has happened to him. And then he affirms the worth of his audience. He says, "King, I'm glad you're here to hear my defense. I believe that because of your understanding of Jewish customs and controversies, you are especially equipped to appreciate what I am going to say." He builds a bridge with Agrippa. He doesn't say, as he might have, "Listen, you corrupt, evil old man: God's going to judge you."

Remember that most of those who hear our witness will probably be ambivalent. They'll be partly hoping that what we're saying is true and partly hoping that it is not. Paul emphasizes the positive and builds on the assumption that the king wants to hear the Good News of Jesus. He is implying that Agrippa has been getting ready all his life to hear this particular case. As we witness, we ought to assume that the other person wants to hear what we want to say.

Next, Paul displays an awareness of Agrippa's need. We can learn from that and tailor our witness to the need of the other person. Luke records Paul telling this story many times, and it's never the same. Sometimes Paul leaves out certain events and adds certain others. I think he does that in direct response to the character of his audience. We can imagine him thinking, "Because of who you are, I'm going to put in this part and leave out that part." I think it's helpful to put our own witness together like that—in modules, if you will, portions you can stick in or leave out, depending on your listeners. Paul seems to do that.

Paul's witness is personal. He tells Agrippa where he has come from. He seems to say, "Listen. Have I been a religious Jew? Have I been a persecutor of Christians? Let me tell you about it. I have punished Christians, even voted to have them killed." It's not unlike the kind of witness you hear at an AA meeting. Members always begin their witness by saying, "You think you've been a drunk. Let me tell you my story. I was the worst drunk you'll ever meet." The rationale is that if somebody that seemingly hopeless can be changed by the power of God, there is hope for everyone else.

Finally, Jesus Christ is at the center of Paul's witness. Paul does not say that on the Damascus Road he had some new intellectual insight. Rather, Jesus Christ interrupted his life, and after that he was not disobedient to Him; his life was different. Then Paul proceeds to describe who this Jesus is. He was crucified and raised from the dead. He is God's Messiah, and if the king has read the prophets and Moses, he knows that this is true.

But the bottom line is, of course, the purpose of witness. It's to get the other person to meet the One who has changed your life. King Agrippa is clever enough to perceive Paul's purpose. Festus, the governor, doesn't understand what's going on. He says, "Paul, you've flipped. Your great learning has driven you mad." But the king understands. He accuses Paul of using this brief time to make him a Christian. "Are you trying to convert me?" We might paraphrase Paul's reply to say, "You bet your boots I am. You found me out." He tells the king how much he wishes that not only he, but all the noble and privileged people that fill the hall, could be just like him, except for his chains. Jesus told His disciples He would make them fishers of men. Witnessing is a kind of fishing, and the purpose of a witness is to catch fish. The purpose is to provide an opportunity for the other person to meet the Jesus who can change his or her life.

Witnessing requires patience. Paul waited two years for this particular opportunity. He expected it and he anticipated it. He was thinking, praying, writing, and working to prepare for this opportunity. As we said, witnessing is not like teaching or delivering a sermon. It is telling about your own experience with God. In this instance, King Agrippa is certainly intrigued, but we don't know what effect Paul's witness had on him ultimately. That's often true for us. We have to leave the results to God. We are patient, we wait for God's time, we seize that opportunity, and we tell what's happened to us.

CHAPTER NINETEEN

Picnics in the Storm

ACTS 27

Chapter 27 is one of my favorite chapters in the Bible. It's
not a chapter of complicated doctrines. It presupposes
that God is and that He intervenes in human history, even in a
disaster. It is a chapter that provides us with a wonderful model for
the living of life. The whole theme of the Bible is that God is with
His people in the good and the bad times, and in that sense it is a
manual for us for living our own lives.

Chapter 27 reminds us that God is with us in disaster. All of us
have disasters. How have you handled past disasters? How will you
handle those that will inevitably come in the months and years
ahead? The chapter begins with the first leg of Paul's journey to
Rome, accompanied by his friends Luke and Aristarchus, the
centurion Julius, his guards, and a squad of soldiers. The first ship
takes Paul from Caesarea to Myra, by way of Sidon. There the
party boards an Egyptian grain ship for the voyage to Rome. From
the very beginning, Luke observes that "the winds were against

us." Those unfavorable winds continue and, in addition, winter is coming upon them. Winter is a bad time to be sailing the Mediterranean on an old ship such as theirs.

Does the fact that "the winds were against them" seem surprising? Wasn't Paul God's hand-picked missionary to Rome? How could the winds be against him? We're reminded again that there is no guarantee that the winds of life won't be against us—believer or unbeliever. Whether we are on some errand of evil or some work of mercy, we're all subject to the same winds, but we need not go where the wind takes us. We have the opportunity to set our sails and reach our chosen destination.

We learn our behaviors and attitudes from models. Psychologists, for example, are discovering that some types of animal behavior are not innate at all. Monkeys taken from their mothers at a very young age, having had no experience of being mothered, don't know what to do with their own young. Mothering apparently is a learned skill. All of us learn behavior patterns from the primary people in our lives who provide us with models.

Most of that life-modeling is nonverbal. Someone told me about identical twin brothers who lived in the same town where one was a pastor and one a physician. One Monday morning, the doctor ran into someone who said, "That was a marvelous sermon you preached last Sunday." "No, no," the doctor protested, "you've got the wrong man. That was my brother. He preaches and I practice." As a preacher, I'm sorry to admit that usually we learn more from those who are practicing then we do from those who are preaching.

For the most part, we learn how to handle disaster from models. We have learned to handle life's storms constructively or destructively. In any disaster, major or minor, financial, medical or physical, we have learned some pattern of behavior. Let's say, for example, you are driving on a lonely mountain road at 2:00 A.M. and you run out of gas. There are no other cars and no gas station for miles. What learned behavior would you bring to that disaster situation? Let's make this a multiple-choice question with the following options:

(1) You can crumple or fold. You simply go to pieces and become hysterical.

(2) You can blame someone. That's one of the great perks in marriage. You always have someone to blame. You can say, "Honey, if you had just put gas in the car as I told you, this wouldn't have happened." It's great to have someone else to blame. During your youth you can say that what's wrong with you is your parents. When you're mature, the younger generation is causing the problems of the world.

(3) You can blame yourself. This is the thing I tend to do. When disaster hits, I say, "Larson, this time you have really surpassed yourself in dumbness. How could you let this happen?" This kind of breast-beating and self-berating doesn't help the situation one bit.

(4) You can pretend the disaster is not happening. You say, "I think I'll take a nap. It may all be over when I wake up." It's a way of handling disaster by dropping out. You can put on your headset and go jogging. You're in your own bubble, transported to your own world, and you leave all unpleasantness behind.

(5) You can use a chemical solution—drink a little booze, take a few pills, smoke some pot. That won't change the circumstances, but you can be oblivious to them, at least for a time.

(6) Frantic effort. This is not a bad plan. Perhaps you are an organizer like my wife. She sees a better way to do everything. You get organized to save yourself. Perhaps you can send up smoke signals from that lonely road in the mountains and get help. You have a plan of action for every disaster.

Those are all viable options, but I prefer the one Paul models for us in his shipwreck. He says, "This is terrible. The ship's going to go down. But before it happens, let's have a picnic. You haven't eaten for a while. Sit down and take some nourishment." While the ship is plunging and rocking he organizes a picnic lunch. "Somebody pass the pumpernickel. Where's the salami? Who's got the ketchup? Open the wine." And they all sat down and ate and felt encouraged in the midst of this disaster at sea.

I can think of any number of disasters our family has gotten into over the years, most of them connected to boat trips. One summer we took our houseboat several thousand miles from New Jersey up to Montreal and back. We had many narrow escapes along the way, often as a result of my ineptness. Three members of the family would invariably say what Oliver Hardy always said, "Now, see what a fine mess you've gotten us into, Stanley." But one member of our family was an unfailing encourager who always said, "Listen, it's not so bad. We're going to make it. Let's fix some cocoa and relax." His response was like Paul's. "Let's have a picnic in the storm."

Mark Twain once said, "I'm an old man and I have seen a lot of troubles in my lifetime that never happened." In the midst of disaster, worrying is like driving your car with the emergency brake on. It is counterproductive. How much we in the church need authentic models who can demonstrate to the world a constructive way of dealing with misfortune. We have an opportunity as a church to witness to the world, not through sermons, but through the lives of people who can function with confidence when the winds are against them.

Paul does try first of all, however, to avert the disaster. The winds are against them and Paul cautions Julius, the centurion, in whose charge he is, against continuing. He says, "I'm an old shipboard traveler, and I know what the winds are like this time of the year. Let's postpone our journey. Let's stay here in Fair Havens for the winter." Since he was not a professional sailor, his advice was ignored. The centurion listened instead to the captain and to the ship's owner.

We are moving into a time when we are becoming increasingly wary of trusting only the professionals. Our local paper recently interviewed Jonas Salk, the discoverer of the polio vaccine. He was asked about his newest venture, which is a think-tank in La Jolla. He revealed that he was never trained in most of the disciplines he pursued—microbiology, epidemiology. Now he's into philosophy. He calls himself an amateur, which means, according to Salk, that he has learned enough to ask the right questions. We're beginning to take professional amateurs more seriously these days. That's what Paul was, and had they listened to him, disaster would have been avoided.

Taking the advice of the professionals, the travelers sail from port, only to run into violent storms. In an effort to save the ship, they throw overboard first the cargo and then the tackle of the ship. It is at this point that Luke, the physician who is recording this story of the early church, once more points out Paul's humanity. Again we are aware that the treasure of the gospel is in very frail earthen vessels—cracked pots like you and me. Before Paul acts constructively, he has to say, "I told you so. If you had listened to me we wouldn't have sailed at all." But then he encourages them. The Lord has told him that he will reach Rome, and therefore they will all be saved. "Take heart," he says. "There will be no loss of life but only of the ship."

Shortly thereafter, they suspect they are nearing land and, fearing to crash on the rocks, the sailors get ready to abandon the ship. Paul intervenes again: "Unless these men stay on the ship, you cannot be saved." This time the captain and the centurion listen to him. They are convinced enough to cut away the ropes of the lifeboats. It is at the end of this violent, storm-tossed night that Paul suggests they eat. He takes bread and begins to eat, and seeing his example, so do they all. This kind of witness in the midst of disaster is what authentic faith is all about.

The person of faith is constructive, even when the winds are against him or her. The doctor who can encourage his patient in the face of serious illness is that kind of person. Nobody can predict who's going to make it through some dread disease. But a physician of the soul can communicate his belief that you're going to recover. Sir William Osler, the great North American pioneer physician, has said, "Most of our patients get well because they have faith in the doctor's faith in the cure." The doctor might say,

"There's a storm in your life but I think you're going to make it. Let's have a picnic."

We lived on an island in south Florida for six years before we moved to Seattle, Washington. One of the biggest hurricanes we experienced during our stay there hit on a day when our family had just returned from overseas. We arrived at our house to find that most of our neighbors had evacuated the island in response to hurricane warnings. We weren't sure what to do, but it was too late to leave. We rushed out and bought candles and foodstuffs and tape for the windows. While the rest of us were making these frantic preparations, our youngest son had other plans. "We don't usually get waves like this in the Gulf of Mexico," he said. "I think I'll get my surfboard out and try a bit of surfing while we wait for the storm." Crazy as it sounded, we all relaxed. If Mark could take off to surf in those enormous waves, it couldn't be so bad. Why waste good waves just because a hurricane is coming?

A friend of mine tells a wonderful story about his mother. He grew up during the depression and the family income barely covered the basics of food and clothing. "My mother's attitude was a saving grace," said my friend. "When things were at their worst, she would go out shopping, against my father's wishes and incurring his anger, to buy a great big gorgeous new hat. She would come home wearing that hat like a flag, and it said to us that our poverty was temporary. My mother's hat somehow gave us all hope that things were going to get better." That's one kind of picnic in a storm.

What can we learn from Paul about an authentic Christian life style when disasters come? First of all, Paul believes that God can work in disasters. He expected Him to work. God can work even when we have been disobedient and gone against clear guidance, as Paul's superiors did. Robert Schuller of Crystal Cathedral has coined a profound phrase. He says that there is something wrong with every great idea. When you bring your great new idea to some committee or board, you can expect at least one person to say, "That will never work." That's a Schullerism, and I commend it to you. Here's a Larsonism: "There is something potentially great in every disaster." In every disaster you will ever be in, God has a gift for you. Claim it. Say, "God, I want the gift you have for me in this disaster."

Someone has said, "Life may be a shipwreck, but it's a sin not to sing in the lifeboats." In any personal disaster, it seems to me you have two choices. You can be like a clam and close your shell and dig in to wait out the disaster. Or, you can spread your wings like the eagle and start soaring. They that wait upon the Lord in the times of distress will mount up with the wings of eagles and find the thermals of the Holy Spirit.

Finally, we can have the confidence of Paul. He knows how the game ends and so do we. Have you ever watched a TV replay of a football or basketball game where you've already heard that your beloved team has won? When we see them fumble or the opposition surge ahead, we're unruffled. We can relax because we know how it will all turn out. They're going to win. Life is like that for the Christian. God has assured us we're going to come through, somehow, some way. The course may be difficult and fraught with hardships, but ultimately we're going to make it. We can relax.

When the Boston Celtics were consistently winning, their coach was Red Auerbach. He had a habit that endeared him to his fans and greatly irritated the opposition. At that point in the play when he thought his Celtics had put the game in the bag, beyond the place where the opposition could possibly claim victory, he took out a big, black cigar and lit it. The Celtic fans would start to cheer because Auerbach's cigar meant, "We've got it made."

Now, I don't think God smokes cigars, but we can look to our celestial coach on the sidelines for that assuring sign when we are in the midst of disaster—the sign that says, "You're going to make it. Let's have a picnic." Handling disasters, large or small, is a test of our faith. We are modeling for others our fear or faith, our panic or confidence. When disasters hit, don't waste them. Be the one who says, "Let's have a picnic."

CHAPTER TWENTY

The Great Divide

ACTS 28

The last chapter in Acts marks an end and a beginning. It is the end of the record of the early church; it's the beginning of the church as we know it today. Once wind and fire swept through an Upper Room in a remote province of the Roman Empire. That blaze became a forest fire fanned by a hurricane sweeping across the whole known world and consuming all before it. The one hundred and twenty in that Upper Room at Pentecost grew to tens of thousands in less than one lifetime. We could speak of the twenty-eighth chapter of Acts as a transition chapter.

Paul and the company with him had survived the shipwreck. As the ship broke into pieces, they swam ashore to an island and found themselves on the coast of Malta. They were welcomed by the natives and cared for. These were not Christian people, but they ministered to Paul, Luke, Aristarchus, the soldiers, and the sailors and built a fire to warm them. They offered hospitality, which is a fragrant gift.

It is this kind of instinctive hospitality that has been associated with the church of Jesus Christ through the centuries. Monasteries and convents and countless individual Christians have provided refuge for the homeless and needy of the world. There are many homeless people in America's cities today. One of my dreams is that in each city someone might organize all the unused Christian guest rooms into a pool to house these people. Each of us could put that extra room into the pool for a day or two a month. Then on any given day there would be hundreds of rooms available to anyone in need of shelter. That would be a dramatic and tangible way of expressing our concern for the transient, the stranger, the sojourner.

Paul, having just barely survived a shipwreck, was nevertheless unable simply to sit and do nothing. He insisted on helping his hosts build a fire. He went out and gathered sticks. All of us with the Martha syndrome should be encouraged. You remember that on a visit to the home of Mary and Martha, Jesus rebuked Martha for her preoccupation with serving. Paul was a Martha too. He couldn't bear to be useless. In many parishes where I have visited, especially in some of the small towns, the church exists and thrives because of the Marthas who are baking the casseroles and driving the car pools and opening their guest rooms to strangers.

The whole shipwreck story raises the old question "Why do the righteous suffer?" In a previous chapter, the winds were against Paul's whole company for the entire voyage, which is why they were eventually shipwrecked. We could conclude that God doesn't care about us personally. The winds are against Christian and non-Christian alike. But, as Paul was gathering wood, he was bitten by a deadly snake. He picked it up, thinking it was a stick, which would lead us to think that it was probably frozen stiff. Brought to the fire, the creature began to thaw and promptly bit Paul's hand. However, Paul shook the snake off into the fire and suffered no harm. The point is that while our God is always able to deliver us, He does not always do so. The winds are often against us. But there are times when God does intervene as He did here. Our faith is not a magic shield that protects us, yet our faith does not rest in an impersonal, uncaring God.

As Paul was delivered from this deadly snake bite, those watching the drama went through several reactions. First, they assumed he was a murderer getting his just desserts. He had escaped the shipwreck, only to be killed anyway. When he didn't die, they believed he must be a god. In the Presbyterian church where I grew up, at least once a year the pastor would quote these words. "They say— What do they say? Let them say!" The point is we need not lead our lives under the tyranny of other peoples' evaluations of us. The opinions of these primitive natives about Paul did not change who and what he was.

As sophisticated as we think we are today, we can still operate on that same sort of erroneous assumption that the good prosper. If you are ill or if you are divorced or having marital or financial difficulties, it must be because you are not living the Christian life. Unfortunately, bad things happen to good people; bad things happen to bad people. A genuine Christian theological interpretation of life is that the winds can be against all of us. As Christians, we believe that God is with us in adversity and has the power to deliver us, whether He chooses to or not.

We might entitle the next incident "The Story of the First Medical Mission." Paul and his party were taken into the home of Publius, the leading man of the district. Since several hundred people were given shelter, we can assume it was a very sizable house, the home of a very wealthy man. During the three days that they spent in Publius' home, his father was sick with dysentery and fever. Paul visited him, laid hands on him, and prayed for him, following Jesus' injunction to His disciples in Luke 9:2 to preach and heal. The old man was restored and the news of his recovery spread throughout the island, and the sick from all over the area came and were cured. It's interesting that in the Greek two different words are used to describe the first and then the subsequent healings. The first (*iásato*) means "healed." The other (*etherapeúonto*) means "cured," which is a medical term. Since Dr. Luke was there, we might guess that while Paul was the instrument for the spiritual healing, Luke began a practice there as well, and cured many with his medical skills.

In the course of a research project some years ago, I visited an

unusual hospital called Burswood, situated in Kent County, south
of London. They have two resident physicians on the staff, men
who treat the sick all week long. But on Sunday afternoon in the
chapel, all those who seek healing come forward for the laying on
of hands and for anointing with oil. The service, from the Episcopal Prayer Book, is led by two ordained priests, the same two men
who, as medical doctors, treat these patients through the week.
After the service, they talked to me about the unique role they play
in this unusual healing center. One said, "Whether through spiritual means or medical, only God heals. We make ourselves available to Him for both." This approach to illness is in the tradition of
Luke and Paul and their ministry here at Malta.

Eventually, Paul and his party moved on to their original destination—Rome! They landed at a port city and traveled thirty or
forty miles inland to the great city. While they were still miles
away, they were met by a welcoming committee. The Greek word
used for "meet" implies that they were received like conquering
heroes. About time, I say! In the years since his conversion, poor
Paul had been beaten and stoned, imprisoned, rejected, and mis-
understood. Finally, he was honored. The brethren in Rome had
heard of his arrival and planned an enthusiastic reception for him.
All the wonders of Rome were ahead. We can only guess what that
meant in those days. Today we think of the Via Veneto and pizza
and espresso. But whatever wonders were available at that time,
I'm sure the real stimulus in Rome for Paul was the saints, that
band of Christians who had heard about him and who rejoiced
that he had finally arrived.

In Rome Paul was under house arrest but free to live in his own
quarters and to come and go. He invited the Jewish community to
visit him with the express purpose of giving them a chance to
respond to the message of Jesus and the Kingdom of God. It was
the first opportunity for the Jews in Rome to hear about salvation
through Jesus. The tragedy is that they rejected the message. That
was the beginning of the great divide. Paul read Isaiah 6:9–10 to
them: "Go to this people and say, You shall indeed hear but never
understand, and you shall indeed see but never perceive."

No one really knows Paul's eventual fate. He lived in Rome, we know, for two years. According to the laws then, if someone was charged with a crime and the accuser didn't present formal charges within a two-year period, he was released. We don't know if the Jews from Jerusalem came to Rome to press charges. We can make certain deductions, however. If they did not come, and Paul was therefore released, such triumphant news would certainly have found its way into the epistles. Since it is not mentioned, it is logical to assume that he was tried and convicted, and eventually killed.

As we began this examination of the Book of Acts, I pointed out that the English title is not very accurate. This is not the story of the Acts of the Apostles. It's the story of the Holy Spirit empowering apostolic people. In one sense, what happened to Paul is incidental. He finally brought the Gospel to Rome and then was not heard of again. But the wind and fire of the Holy Spirit continued in and through God's people.

The great divide for the Jews in Rome centered in the choice between religion and Jesus. Paul preached Jesus and they preferred religion. They preferred tradition to the wind and fire of God. They would rather walk around celebrating the memory of God—who He was and what He had done—than experience the present tense of God. A lot of us still have that problem. We remember the way things were ten or twenty years ago and insist that we cannot properly worship without those old traditions. We hang onto them long after they seem to have any relevance for present-day congregations. Often, the Sunday evening service is that kind of a vestigial event. I heard about three women who were discussing their various Sunday evening services. The first complained, "In our church if fifty people attend the Sunday evening service, we're lucky." The second said, "We're fortunate in our church if we get a dozen out." The third dear old saint said, "In our Sunday evening services, every time the minister says, 'Dearly beloved,' I blush."

Why do we hang onto programs that seem to have lost their meaning? Possibly because tradition is safer than the wind and fire of God. The implication here is that the Jews were open-minded. I have a hard time believing that. We're all prejudiced. The only way to know truth is to be aware of your prejudices and discount them. In quoting Isaiah to this group of Jews, Paul was saying to them that they had turned their backs on the Kingdom of God. He went on to say that God was going to use their hardness of heart for good. It would be the means of opening up salvation for the Gentiles. This very rejection of God would open the Good News to all people, because God loves the whole world. God so loved the world—Jews and Gentiles alike—that sometimes even our rejection of Him will be used for good, as happened here.

Because of the great divide that occurred in the first century, Christianity was no longer a Jewish sect. It became a world faith, and you and I are part of it. That movement had its beginnings there in Rome. The Roman church was apparently largely a Gentile church. The Bible says there were saints in Caesar's household. The Christians had infiltrated the home of the emperor. He was surrounded by secret saints. We learn from later epistles that there were Christian saints in the praetorian guard. We can understand how that might have happened. For Paul's two years of house arrest, he had guards living with him. We can only imagine what a life-changing experience that must have been for the guards. In our own century, when Dietrich Bonhoeffer, the great German martyr, was imprisoned by the Nazis, his guards had to be changed constantly, because he kept converting them. I'm sure that was the situation with Paul's guards.

The great divide between religion or Jesus is a timely issue. How open are we to what the omnipresent God is saying to us individually, and as a church? We have so many ways of making our focus something other than Jesus. Is it tradition or Jesus? Is it theology or Jesus? Is it social action or Jesus? Is it good works or Jesus? Is it piety or Jesus? Then there is the Jesus-plus gospel that we hear on every side. It's Jesus-plus my politics, Jesus-plus my ethics, Jesus-plus my life style. Recently I watched a famous TV preacher with an unusual pitch. He was asking his audience to send money to support his ministry, and in return they would receive a faith-partner's kit—a special Bible prepared by the preacher, jewelry to wear, a whole bag of religious items. How impossible it is to imagine the Apostle Paul offering somebody a faith-partner kit! I can't imagine him preaching a Jesus-plus gospel, Jesus-plus some gimmick, or Jesus-plus some technique.

We can make Jesus an appendage. We invite Him to help at difficult times in our life. We need His help in our home, our business, or our profession. But whatever our vocations, we Christians are meant to be, first of all, ambassadors for the Kingdom of God. Horace Mann, the famous liberal educator of the nineteenth century, gave a graduation address at Antioch College in 1859 in which he said, "Be ashamed to die until you have won some victory for humanity." I would paraphrase that to say, "Be ashamed to die until you have invested yourself in some part of the Kingdom and seen some results blossom and grow." The Kingdom is our number one priority.

The great divide centers in the person of Jesus. He is also the great unifier. When we have met Him, then the divisions that normally separate us become much less important.

There's a story I love about Cyrus, King of Persia, whose armies were constantly harassed by a rebel chieftain named Cagular. Exasperated, he finally dispatched his whole army to capture the chieftain and his wife and family. They were brought to the capitol for trial and execution. Face to face with the strong, skilled warrior, Cyrus thought better of his original intention. He said, "Cagular, if I were to save your life, what would you do?" "Oh, King, I would serve you the rest of my days," was the reply. Next, Cyrus asked, "What would you do if I spared the life of your wife?" Cagular answered, "Your Majesty, if you spared the life of my wife, I would die for you." After this exchange, Cyrus decided on an alliance with Cagular, and put him in charge of the troops at his southern border.

On the journey home, Cagular began to discuss this extraordinary audience with his wife. Commenting on the riches of Cyrus's court, he asked, "Did you notice the marble courtyard? Did you see the magnificent silver armor on the soldiers? Did you see the solid gold throne Cyrus sat on?" His wife said, "I saw none of those things." "You didn't? What did you see?" he queried. She said, "I saw only the face of the man who said he would die for me." That's a picture that occupies your whole horizon. If you and I have seen the love of God in Jesus, who has died for us, we can work together for His Kingdom, united with all kinds of Christians from a wide variety of positions and traditions.

As we finish Acts we leave Paul in an uncharacteristic state. He is now comfortable. He is respected. He's a middle-class tentmaker living in Rome, entertaining friends, speaking freely. There's no more harassment, no more problems and no more persecution. For two years, except for his guards, he lives much as you and I would. It's hard for me, a comfortable, well-fed, middle-class Christian, to identify with the Apostle Paul of the first twenty-seven chapters. He was stoned, beaten, and persecuted. For most of us, such hardships are not yet within our experience. His life in Rome is settled, secure and comparatively uneventful. That's our situation. But Paul's message and effectiveness continued undiminished. He preached the Word with passion in season and out of season. His circumstances did not change the man nor his message.

We are presented with the same challenge today. Can we as a church survive two thousand years of success? Can we, in the Western world, without the pressure of opposition and persecution, still be empowered and motivated by the wind and fire of the Spirit to be ambassadors for the Kingdom? With God's help, of course we can. May we, like Paul in the final verses of this powerful Book of Acts, welcome all who come, "preaching the Kingdom of God and teaching about the Lord Jesus quite openly."